HARMONY
for
GUITAR

Revised edition

HARMONY
for
GUITAR

Revised edition

LANCE BOSMAN

A Guitar magazine project

Musical New Services

To Sally Mays

Order No MN10095
ISBN 0–7119–2388–4

Distributed by Music Sales Limited
8/9 Frith Street, London W1V 5TZ

Printed and bound in England
by Caligraving Limited
Thetford, Norfolk

CONTENTS

INTRODUCTION

Before taking up a study of a particular branch of melody and harmony, a preparatory range of general ground must be covered. Our well-known scales and chords, for all the colouring and embellishments they have acquired in different musical idioms, have long-established origins. Tracing these from a traditional basis will offer a step-by-step knowledge of the makeup of classical guitar pieces in the guitar repertoire, and provide openings to investigate later fields of music in which the instrument plays a part.

Viewing fundamentals of music across a broad front has another advantage in that comparative assessments may be drawn. Not only can the characteristics of scales and chords be compared directly, one against another, but across idioms too. There is no reason why a chord sequence used in much the same way for classical and modern styles of composition cannot be introduced in both lights - old and new. For instance, where the chords supporting folk songs, blues and popular songs bear similarities to those in classical harmony, different treatments of those progressions can be illustrated side by side. One step further, standard jazz progressions are derived from centuries-old common chord sequences. A knowledge of simple chords is easily extended to embrace the ornaments peculiar to jazz harmony. Many old note patterns and traditional chords crop up in formal contemporary music. These, too, can be examined from both sides. Where they have been modified to suit a recent style, their later uses will be dealt with at a stage where elements of modern music are the main consideration.

Then scales and the structure and layout of chords for classical guitar pieces, song accompaniments, jazz and modern music are the main topics over the following chapters. In approaching these, most components are first shown reduced to their essentials so that they can be seen free of trappings and possible distractions. They are then placed in excerpts from live music to demonstrate their practical applications and effects. Explanatory notes accompanying the excerpts are concerned mainly with the device under discussion, but may also refer to others covered earlier, and sometimes include points of interest regarding the overall shape and ornamentation of the composition. When the relationship of certain scale notes and chords cannot be fully conveyed within a short phrase, a complete section of a work is given, and occasionally a whole piece. In the latter, chords and notes which are placed at detached positions yet have strong relationships may be fully appreciated. Also, because they appear in their entirety, these examples capture more the flavour and atmosphere that their note combinations generate.

The importance of listening to and absorbing the sound of each example cannot be stressed enough. Words and illustrations help, but sound must be heard. Playing the examples twice over will overcome pitfalls in reading and so allow more concentration to be given to the aural side.

Rules, the do's and don't's for chord setting and the organisation of parts in classical harmony, are kept to a minimum. Rather than a textbook geared for exams, the intention here is to assist the player at home wishing to understand classical harmony and thereby improve interpretation through recognition of musical phrases and the harmony and decorations which emphasise their contours and conclusions. These classical resources plus others from the 20th century will offer a fair cross-section of harmony to develop ideas that arise for instrumental pieces and accompaniments.

L.B.
January 1978

1: THE NATURE OF SCALES

When listening to or casting your eye across a completed composition, it's often difficult to pinpoint the initial ideas from which it stemmed. It may have been prompted by a stray wisp of melody that took hold in the composer's mind. Then again, the composer may not have waited for ideas to arise but sought them, shaping a group of notes into a melodic pattern. In either case, the initial idea, the germ of that composition held a potential for growth. The notes chosen for its development may not have been particularly related outside that composition; or they could have been drawn from one of many closely related series or *scales* in circulation.

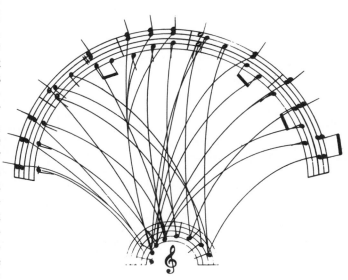

Assuming that the music was composed mainly with the notes of a known scale, it may well be asked, why was that scale picked, was there something special about it? The answer may be simply because it was the most fashionable scale at the time. Equally, it may have been chosen with the knowledge that its air of forcefulness, restraint or whatever characteristics it possessed, would lend themselves most readily to the style and mood of the envisaged work.

Our popular scales have endured through centuries of diverse musical styles. Alongside these, others have sprung up quite different in makeup and sound. One of the traditional scales would probably be chosen for a folk song or an instrumental piece following conventional patterns and harmonised with everyday chords. A later type with an unusual array of steps would be considered more suitable for setting a composition modern in outlook and sound. In order to assess the individual characteristics of scales they are best observed not in isolation but from a comparative viewpoint. From there the construction and character of one can be noted and then compared with those of other scales both directly and through melodies based on them.

First to be singled out are three from a long standing family called the *modes*. These scales, the oldest in western music, have played an important role in folk song and arise from time to time in 20th century music. Following them is the comparatively modern *whole-tone* scale, and after that two *pentatonic* scales whose origins are deep and widespread in European and oriental melodies.

Ex. 1 The modal scales

Ionian C - C¹ — Tonic 2 3 4 5 6 7 tonic, C

Dorian D - D¹ — Tonic, D

Phrygian E - E¹ — Tonic, E

Lydian F - F¹ — Tonic, F

Mixolydian G - G¹ — Tonic, G

Aeolian A - A¹ — Tonic, A

The modal scales became established in Europe through plainsong — an early religious vocal form, and the songs of mediaeval minstrels. Of the six modes shown in Ex.1, the *Ionian* (now the major), the *Dorian* and the *Aeolian* continue as a basis for folk songs and instrumental compositions, and the *Phrygian* as a basis for flamenco.

Each scale has eight notes and is given a Greek name. The first notes of the scales are called their *tonics*, and the notes following the tonics ascend as *degrees:* tonic - 2nd degree - 3rd degree, etc.* At the end of the scales the tonics recur but they are now eight degrees or an *octave* higher. These upper tonics are the starting notes for the scales to recommence their ascent at a higher pitch. Hence the compass of the Ionian, for example is from its tonic C to octave C'.

A mode omitted from the range here is the *Locrian* with a tonic B. For reasons that will be explained later, this mode is rarely used in instrumental work and never for folk song. Our concern at present is with the Ionian, Dorian and Aeolian, the modes on which a vast corpus of folk song and instrumental work is based. The characteristics of these three scales will now be compared directly one against the other, then through melodies based on them.

Ex. 2

Ionian — t t st t t t st

Dorian — t st t t t st t

Aeolian — t st t t st t t

Although similar in appearance, the scales in Ex.2 have different characters. The Ionian could be described as decisive in ascent when heard alongside the Dorian and Aeolian. The reason why these scales differ in character is because they have individual layouts of tones and semitones.

Comparing their tone-semitone orders, notice that the Ionian is the only scale of the three with a semitone from its 7th degree (B) to upper tonic (C). Propelled with a last-moment impetus·across this final, short semitone step, the scale ends decisively on its upper tonic (indicated by the top arrow in Ex.3).

* In modal composition the tonics of the above scales are called 'finals'. So the Dorian has a 'final' D, etc.

Ex. 3 Ionian Mode

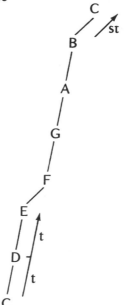

In addition to the Ionian's semitone step from its 7th degree to upper tonic, there is another factor that contributes to its forthright character. From its lower tonic C to 3rd degree E, are two whole-tone steps. The initial momentum created in striding these whole-tones sets the scale firmly in motion on an equidistant footing in preparation for the rest of its ascent (indicated by the lower arrow in Ex.3).

How different are the characters of the Dorian and Aeolian modes! Whereas the Ionian gains momentum in its initial steps, the Dorian and Aeolian are restrained at their departures by having to take a shorter step at their 2nd to 3rd degrees (indicated by the lower arrows in Ex.4).

Ex. 4

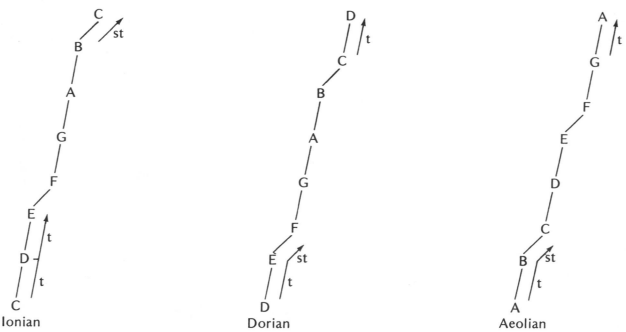

Furthermore, the Dorian and Aeolian must cross a whole-tone from their 7th degrees to upper tonics. At this stage, the final leg of their ascents, they cross this whole-tone step as though reluctant to arrive at their destination (indicated by the upper arrows in Ex.4).

4

These characteristics are reflected in melodies based on the scales. If the tempo of the song is fast they may not be so apparent, but in slow moving tunes such as those in Ex.5, they are readily detectable. The three phrases in this example are each based on a different mode but follow the same pattern. Though the latter two faithfully trace the Ionian's shape, they do so from their own source of notes, the Aeolian and Dorian modes.

Ex. 5

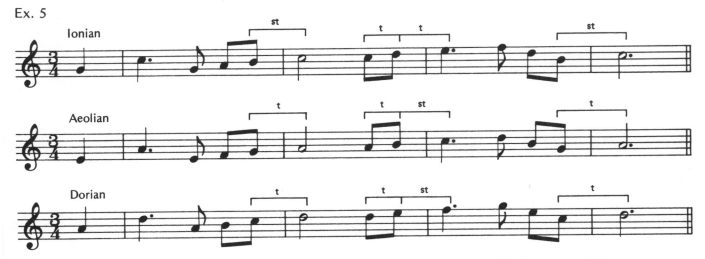

Play the Ionian version a couple of times or so, listening for its compulsive upward step from the 7th degree B to tonic C, and its assertive whole-tone steps from C upwards through D and E. Then compare this with the other two versions, listening for their reticent whole-tone steps to their tonics, and the restraint imposed by the semitones at their 2nd to 3rd degrees.

From these brief phrases to a broader comparison with complete tunes, the following songs are based on the Ionian, Dorian and Aeolian (Exs.6-8).

Ex. 6 Soldier, Soldier - Ionian

With a march-like tempo, the melody in Ex.6 emphasises the subject of the lyric — a soldier, who as later verses reveal, is about to make himself scarce. Listen how the line steps nimbly by whole-tone steps from the tonic C, through the second and 3rd degrees, D and E. Ending as decisively as it began, the melody is drawn smartly to rest via its final semitone step.

In marked contrast, the following Dorian and Aeolian melodies (Exs.7 and 8), typify so many of the ballads based on these modes. Observe in the notation, and listen for, the reticent ascents of 1½ tones (a), and pensive whole-tone steps (b).

Ex. 7 Scarborough Fair - Dorian

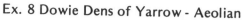

Ex. 8 Dowie Dens of Yarrow - Aeolian

There lived a la-dy in the— West. Some said she had no mar - row. She was
Am
G

court-ed by a gent-le-man, and the plough-mans lad in Yar - row.
Am
Em
G
Am

Tempo of course has much to do with the mood of a song. A slow Ionian lament would engender the same degree of sadness pervading 'Scarborough Fair'. Equally, there are up-tempo Dorian and Aeolian tunes which are as jaunty as 'Soldier won't you marry me'? For instance, the Dorian 'Drunken Sailor' could hardly be described as lacking zest. But the aim here is to show what effect the characteristics of these modes impart should the tempo allow them full vent.

Neo-modality

The modal scales have not passed the notice of composers of solo instrumental and orchestral music. Through their innovations, notably those that occurred around the turn of this century, the modes have enjoyed a revival. *Neo-modality*, of which Claude Debussy and Ralph Vaughan Williams were two leading exponents, has archaic and exotic elements within essentially modern settings. Episodes or extended passages of modal melodies, sometimes drawn from folk song or recalling mediaeval music, are merged with modern harmonies to conjure up a certain atmosphere, combining the old with the new.

The major scale

From the modal system, two scales emerged that were to become the most celebrated in Western music. One of these, the *minor*, will be dealt with in due course, the other, shown in Ex.9, is the *major* scale.

Ex. 9 C major

1 t 2 t 3 st 4 t 5 t 6 t 7 st 8

During the 17th century the major scale became accepted as a principal basis for European music. Long before its general recognition as the 'major' it was used by minstrels who knew it as the Ionian mode. Through their songs and other secular music, the major's popularity spread to such an extent that musicians sharpened and flattened certain notes in other modal scales so that their tone-semitone orders would tally with that of the major. By the late 17th century, the major (and minor) had overshadowed and superseded the modal system as the main basis for western composition.

The major scale in Ex.9 has a tonic C, the note from which it receives its letter name, C major. It has two semitone steps, the first at the 3rd to 4th degrees, and the second at the 7th degree to upper tonic. The other notes ascend as tones. It is important to remember this sequence as there will constant reference to it later.

When this scale was examined earlier as the Ionian mode, it was pointed out that its initial two whole-tone and final semitone steps are factors that contribute to its forceful ascent. In addition to these, it exerts other forces which result from certain of its notes beckoning one another from adjacent and detached points. These notes are the tonic, 4th and 5th degrees (Ex.10).

Ex. 10 C major

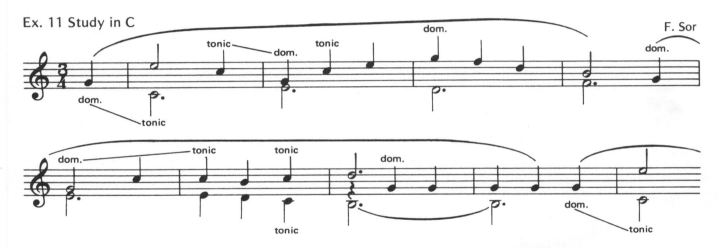

By far the most important note in the major scale is its first note or *tonic*. As the anchor of the scale or a composition based on the scale, the tonic is usually placed at or near the beginning of a melody or bass line; it is also the note that the lines intersect and rest upon during their course; and often the note on which they end.

Closely allied to the tonic is the 5th degree or *dominant*. A kind of magnetic link exists between these two notes, an affinity that manifests itself in melodies and bass lines, lulling them to and fro between their tonic and dominant notes (Ex.11).

Ex. 11 Study in C   F. Sor

The more facile the music, the more evident is the push-pull of its tonic and dominant notes. In Ex.11, a simple study for guitar, the interaction of the tonic and dominant motions the two lines forward either by direct leaps between these points, or through intervening scale notes. Where the tonic and dominant are joined directly, their attraction is concentrated into one decisive movement. As seen here (and in Ex.6) this movement often occurs at the beginning of a phrase as an *upbeat* or *anacrusis*, a springboard for the music's departure. A 5-1 progression is also placed at the end of a phrase where its decisive leap from dominant to tonic emphasises the latter note as the central point of the melody or bass line.

The third most important note in the major scale is the 4th degree or *subdominant*. This note acts as a stepping stone for the melody, though more often a bass line, in its journey to the dominant. The bass line may also side-step the dominant and pivot instead on the subdominant, and from there return to the tonic (bars 3-4, Ex.12).

Ex. 12 Bass line in C major

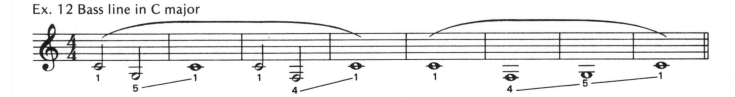

Comprising only the tonic, subdominant and dominant, the bass line in Ex.12 is typical of many underlying classical studies and folk song accompaniments. In its unadorned form here, it is rigid and far from novel, but its movements are nevertheless positive and convey a strong sense of direction. Upon this sequence and its variations many chord progressions will later be built and simple studies set from them.

The subdominant and dominant along with the other major scale degrees are named according to either their relationship with each other, or by their disposition to the tonic. Strangely enough, the subdominant does not derive its name from its proximity to the dominant, but through its relationship with the tonic: as the dominant is four steps above the tonic (1-5), the 'sub' dominant is four steps below it (4-8), Ex.13.

Ex. 13 C major

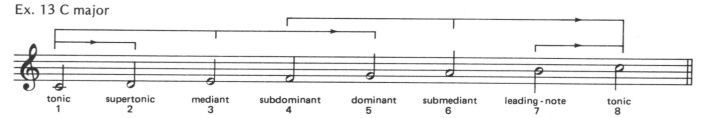

tonic	supertonic	mediant	subdominant	dominant	submediant	leading-note	tonic
1	2	3	4	5	6	7	8

Of the remaining scale notes, the 2nd degree or *supertonic* follows the tonic; the 3rd degree or *mediant* lies midway between the tonic and dominant; the 6th degree or *submediant* lies midway between the subdominant and upper tonic; and the 7th degree or *leading-note* leads directly to the tonic.

The concept of organising a melody or harmonic progression around a tonic or recognisable parent tone is known as *tonality*. A composition is *tonal* if it is assigned a particular tone to serve as its central reference point. The major scale is particularly suitable for tonal writing; more a hierarchy of notes than simply a sequence of tones and semitones, the major's dominant, subdominant and leading-note all help to reinforce the status of the tonic as the principal note in the composition.

Though tonality was once regarded as fundamental to Western composition, it is no longer so. Tonality has been deliberately rejected in some quarters and upheld in others, both in its traditional forms and modified with new techniques. Many of these techniques were formulated in the late 19th century. Composers at that time, finding their inherited scales and chords inadequate for the expression of new ideas, augmented existing resources with all manner of melodic embellishments and complex harmony.

Partly as an extension, and partly in reaction to these developments, a new style of composition emerged in the early 20th century called Impressionism. Musically, Impressionism is characterised by lush, elusive harmonies, and sometimes incorporates melodies with folk song, oriental or ancient allusions. One technical aspect of Impressionism is the subordination of the tonic by the deliberate omission of the leading-note — hence the absence of the force incurred by the semitone step to the tonic. Two scales without semitone leading-notes are the Dorian and Aeolian. Revived in neo-modal form these are prominent elements in Impressionistic music. Two other scales used also with whole-tone steps preceding their tonics are the *pentatonic*, a traditional type, and the *whole-tone* scale, of comparatively recent origin.

Ex. 14 Whole - tone scale on C

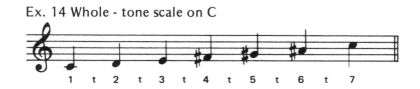

| 1 | t | 2 | t | 3 | t | 4 | t | 5 | t | 6 | t | 7 |

Unlike the major and modal scales, the whole-tone scale has no semitone steps, therefore it has no assertive or restraining characteristics. Compare the sound of Ex.14 with C major, and notice that this scale lacks a leading-note thrust, and that there is little liaison between its 1st and 5th notes.

Progressing with equidistant steps, it's relatively easy to begin the whole-tone scale on any note. Select one note from the scale and simply mark out six whole-tone steps from that. Should the starting note be D instead of C, the scale would ascend as: D, E, F sharp, G sharp, A sharp, C, D. With these notes plus those in Ex.15, a whole-tone scale can be constructed on any note.

Ex. 15 Whole-tone scale on A

Played slowly and softly the whole-tone scale could be described as somewhat eerie in sound. Some 20th century composers have sought to capture this effect by arranging chords and melodies to progress in whole-tone steps. Generally the scale does not form the entire basis for such compositions, but is used for brief or extended passages along with other modern devices (Ex.16).

Ex. 16 Nocturno   F. Moreno Torroba

But this is only one side of the whole tone scale. In an animated mood, a whole-tone melody can reveal a hard, even aggressive nature. In just such a mood, Ex.17 is based entirely on the whole-tone scale on A.

Ex. 17 Portrait of two scallywags   L.B.

Two voice parts, a spiky melody and an erratic bass line reveal a spirited side to the whole-tone scale. Angular and mobile, the melody is tonally vague. It is as though its agitated movements are seeking the stability of an anchoring note, but are denied it due to the absence of a dominant and leading-note. However, a keynote of a sort is simulated by sounding the open bass string A and allowing it to sustain over the beginning of each phrase.

Pentatonic scales

As its name suggests, a *pentatonic* scale has five notes. There are different types of pentatonic scales, some indigenous to oriental music, and others, of which two are shown in Ex. 18, serve also as a basis for European folksongs.

Ex. 18a Pentatonic on G   Ex. 18b Pentatonic on A

Though the scales in Exs.18 have different starting notes and individual orders of 1½ and one-tone steps, they are nevertheless interrelated. In Ex.18a the first step is a tone. On the second note of this scale Ex.18b begins. From this common point both scales have over their following five notes the same order of 1½ tone and one-tone steps. So really one scale is a continuation of the other. In traditional folk songs, though, the scales do not overlap: the melody will keep to the notes of the particular scale on which it is based (Exs.18c-d).

Ex. 18c The true lover's farewell - pentatonic on A

Collected by
Cecil Sharp

The crow is black, dear love you know. It sure - ly would turn
white. If ev - er I prove false to you. Bright day shall turn to night.

Ex. 18d Come all you fair and tender maidens. Pentatonic on G

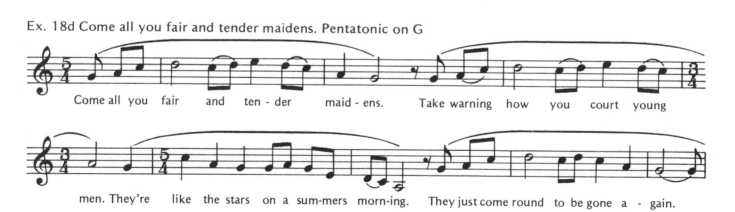

Come all you fair and ten-der maid-ens. Take warning how you court young
men. They're like the stars on a sum-mers morn-ing. They just come round to be gone a - gain.

Despite the pentatonic's limited compass, its disposition of 1½ tones and one-tone steps lends a natural lilt to a melody based on it. 'True Lovers farewell' calls on just one note from outside the scale, the last but one B, because that falls naturally into the descending line. One of many of the versions of the beautiful song, 'Come all you fair and tender maidens', is drawn solely from the pentatonic on G.

Two other pentatonics well worth experimenting with are the *Pelog:* C, D flat, E flat, G, A flat, a scale derived from Javanese music; and the *Kumoi:* A, B, C, E, F sharp, derived from Asian music.

Apart from their folk song connotations and exotic flavour, the simplicity of the pentatonics make them ideal scales for improvisatory ventures on the guitar. And speaking of improvisation, this is the best way of gaining familiarity with the scales discussed, and assessing their individual qualities. To assist this, the principal scales given in this chapter are shown in Ex.19 extended over two octaves. With them are a few suggestions on how improvisation may be approached.

Ex. 19

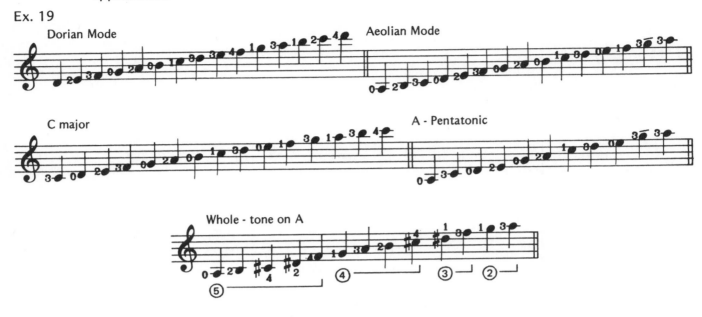

To achieve fluency in improvisation, it is necessary to overcome any hesitation that may result from unfamiliarity with the scales on the guitar. A couple of minutes a day devoted to each will work wonders in ironing out initial fits and starts. Channel impromptu passages into phrases of 'question' and 'response'. The opening phrase in Ex.20, which in this instance is based on the pentatonic, poses a 'question'. After a pause, the answering statement provides a 'response'. Keep the phrases brief at first, back-tracking from time to time as indicated by the curved phrase marks. Then extend the duration of the phrases from four to eight bars. For further examples refer to 'Scarborough Fair' and 'Dens of Yarrow', and notice how their phrase marks define the forward motion of one contour, a kind of breathing in, and the relaxation, a breathing out, of the next.

Ex. 20

Ascending lines usually build up tension, and in descent, release it. These tendencies are emphasised by dynamics for increasing volume — a crescendo, and decreasing it, — a diminuendo. Incentives for composing are to be found in the lines of poetry. The subject and atmosphere of the poem may well suggest a sympathetic musical setting. If the words are light and cheerful in mood then perhaps the music could have a major scale basis; for something sinister or abstract, consider the whole-tone scale; or sad and reflective, the Aeolian or Dorian modes. To project its personality, the melody will require a counterline to enhance its peaks of tension and moments of composure. For that we look to the next chapter.

2: INTERVALS

A single note is struck, and left to ring and fade. It breaks the silence as a monotone, devoid of rhythm and musical context. That note is then played again, but this time another, different one is sounded with it. Those two notes may blend in perfect partnership, relaxed and pleasing to the ear; or they may be two tones that, when paired, obviously don't gel. In a state of restlessness, they could range from a doleful combination to one noticeably agitated.

As an experiment, compare the sounds of the following note pairs. Play the bass note C on the 5th string at the third fret of the guitar. Sustain that note and play over it, its octave C on the 2nd string at the first fret. The combination is an amicable one; those notes were evidently meant to go together. Then play the same bass C but this time against a different higher note, C sharp, a semitone above the first upper C. These notes clash vibrantly. What a radical change from the former, passive combination, C to C, and the conflicting C to C sharp. Their sound is vastly different, and yet in size they differ by a mere semitone.

These are just two contrasting note pairs from a countless number available on the guitar. Many others are neither completely relaxed nor agitated, but sound somewhere in between. The quality of sound, be it pungent, passive or one of the many tonal shades between, will depend on which two notes are struck together. In other words, on the distance of those notes — a distance called an *interval*.

It is the intervals in a melody, the width of its steps and leaps, that determines how angular or flowing that line will be. As small chordal units, intervals are the components of larger chord formations. To understand why chords differ in sound and character, it is necessary to know their constituent intervals and how they are assembled.

First, intervals will be measured, named and placed in categories. Then their sound qualities will be compared directly with one another and discussed in excerpts from classical and modern guitar music.

Measuring and naming intervals

Their numerical size

An interval is measured from its lower to upper note, irrespective of which comes first. In the scale of C major, the interval of the tonic and dominant notes, C-G, has a numerical size of a 5th (Ex.21a). Notice that *both* notes are included in the calculation.

The notes of the 5th in Ex.21b are given a horizontal or *melodic* emphasis: one note follows the other as in melodies. In Ex.21c the notes are given a vertical or *harmonic* emphasis: they are played together as in chords.

Intervals in C major

The following intervals each have a lower note C, and an upper note from the scale of C major (Ex.22).

Ex. 22 Intervals in C major

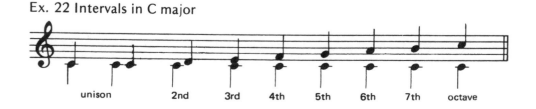

The interval on the far left of Ex.22 has two notes of the same pitch, a *unison*. Normally a unison is notated with two tails connected to one note head, but it may be written as two adjacent notes. The intervals following the unison have a different upper note from the scale of C major: C-D, a 2nd; C-E, a 3rd, etc. Remember that both notes are included in the calculation.

Classifying intervals: major, minor, perfect

Two intervals can be the same size numerically and yet differ in distance. This is because the numerical size states the number of steps — a 2nd, a 3rd, etc, but does not take into account the tones and semitones that lie between those notes. For instance, the interval C-D is a 2nd of one tone. If its upper note is lowered to D flat, it is still a 2nd but now a semitone (C-D flat). As there is a marked difference in sound between a 2nd of a tone, and a 2nd of a semitone, it is necessary to be able to distinguish between them. The wider 2nd, a tone, is classified a *major* 2nd; the smaller 2nd, a semitone, is a *minor* 2nd (Ex.23).

Ex. 23 Major and minor 2nds

Major and minor 3rds

Like 2nds, intervals of 3rds are classified major or minor. These too differ in distance by a semitone. Major 3rds are 2 tones, and minor 3rds are 1½ tones (Exs.24).

Ex. 24a Melodic major and minor 3rds   Ex. 24b Harmonic major and
                                                                      minor 3rds

The difference in sound between a major 3rd and minor 3rd is not so marked when their notes are played melodically (Ex.24a), but heard harmonically as in Ex.24b, it is noticeable. In these, the upper notes of the major 3rds are lowered by a semitone, converting the intervals to minor 3rds. Play them in the order given and you will hear that in comparison to the major 3rds, the accompanying minor 3rds sound subdued.

Perfect intervals: unisons, 4th, 5ths and octaves

Intervals classified 'perfect' are so called because they are considered to be the 'purest' combinations of tones. Perfect intervals are, unisons, octaves and the 4ths and 5ths in Ex.25.

Ex. 25 Perfect intervals

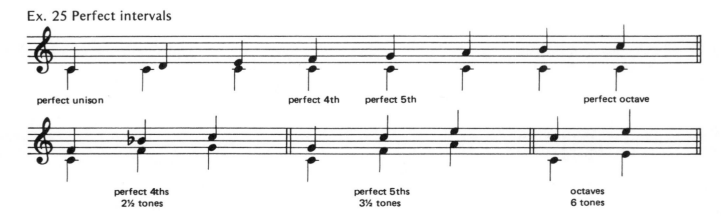

A *unison* is not strictly speaking an interval as there is no distance between its notes; but in practice it is regarded as one, for instance, when two or more voice parts depart from, or converge on its notes. A *perfect 4th* is 2½ tones, and a *perfect 5th* is 3½ tones. (There are also 4ths and 5ths which are not classified perfect but these will be dealt with later). The remaining perfect interval, an *octave* is 6 tones.

Major and minor 6ths and 7ths

Major 6ths are 4½ tones, a semitone bigger than *minor 6ths* of 4 tones (Ex.26a). *Major 7ths* are 5½ tones, and *minor 7ths* are 5 tones (Ex.26b).

Ex. 26a Major and minor 6ths   Ex. 26b Major and minor 7ths

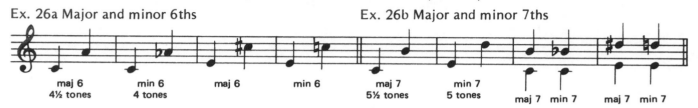

When a major 6th or 7th is converted to a minor 6th or 7th, their change of sound is similar in effect to the conversion of a major 3rd to minor 3rd: the major intervals are more prominent.

Compound intervals

Intervals wider than octaves are *compound* intervals. These are measured in two ways. In the first method, usually adopted for two-part writing, compound intervals are measured and classified as though they were within an octave except that the term 'compound' is sometimes included (Exs.27).

Ex. 27a   Ex. 27b   Ex. 27c   Ex. 27d

A compound major 3rd is an octave (C-C') plus a major 3rd (C-E), Ex.27a. Similarly, a compound major 2nd (Ex.27b) is an octave (C-C') plus a major 2nd (C-D).

In the second method, more applicable to intervals in chords, the numerical size is reckoned in terms of the total number of steps. When a compound major 2nd forms part of a chord it is most likely to be stated as a major 9th — where the upper note is eight steps from the lower one (Ex.27c). An interval of two octaves is a *double-octave* (Ex.27d).

Practical applications

Merging, contrasting or in conflict with their surroundings, the individual sound qualities of intervals cannot readily be assessed in isolation from live musical contexts. But it is possible to concentrate on one or two specific intervals at a time by selecting examples in which they either predominate or are highlighted in some way.

At the opening of this chapter it was pointed out that some intervals are harmonious or passive while others sound agitated or active. Intervals with notes that blend harmoniously are *consonances*. Those in states of agitation are *dissonances*. However, a clear-cut line cannot be drawn through the middle of the interval spectrum separating consonance from dissonance without considering certain factors. Styles of music change and so do composers' and listeners' attitudes to sounds. Some intervals accepted today as consonances were regarded in the past as dissonances. There is also the question of individual response and conditioning. A listener at home with the more astringent styles of 20th century music, would not recoil from those dissonances that might cause other ears, unfamiliar with those forms, to flinch.

Nevertheless, intervals are placed in consonant and dissonant categories as a convenient means for definition and application. First to be considered in a practical light are the consonances. These are: major and minor 3rds and 6ths, unisons, octaves, and perfect 4ths and 5ths.

Major and minor 3rds and 6ths

Pleasant in sound and unobtrusive in effect, 3rds and 6ths are the principal intervals in standard harmony. Consecutively linked they form smooth chains of blending note pairs. Placed one on the other they merge as the familiar major and minor chords used in arrangements of popular music and folk song accompaniments (Ex.28a) and the harmony for classical instrumental compositions (Ex.28b).

Ex. 28a Müss Ich Denn (Must I Then)

An instrumental arrangement of a traditional German folk song, the upper line of Ex.28a wends smoothly along with melodic steps of 2nds and leaps of 3rds. Supporting these on accented beats are lower notes a 3rd or 6th down. There are also four octaves, one at the beginning and one near the end of the melody to emphasise the tonic C; and two between to give depth to the bass line. At the end of the last bar a unison draws the melody, centre line and bass together on the tonic in preparation for the next verse (see Ex.143).

Ex. 28b Waltz   D. Aguado

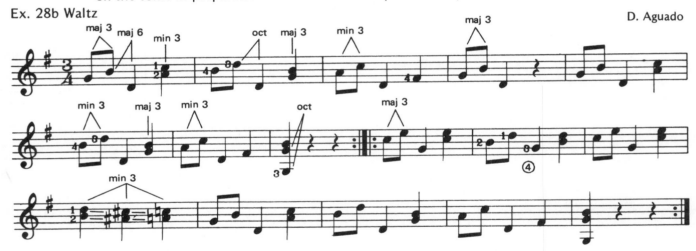

In much the same style, Ex.28b, a simple study for guitar, has 3rds and 6ths arranged horizontally as an easy going melody. Every so often 3rds are set vertically to double the line and bring it out a little.

Perfect 4ths and 5ths

Compared to the pleasant sound of 3rds and 6ths, perfect intervals are stark. In the following fantasia no other intervals could quite give the feeling of distance and sparseness as the 4ths, 5ths and octaves dividing its lines.

Ex. 29 Fantasia   Luys de Narvāez 1538
                                                   (transcribed by J. D. Roberts)

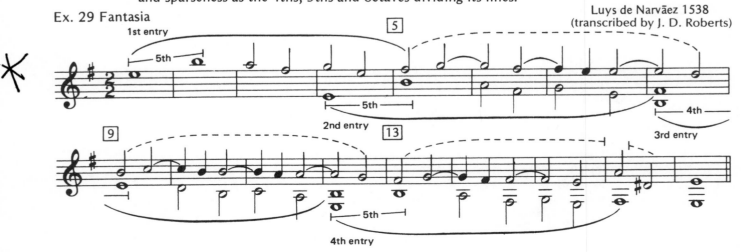

Despite its apparent simplicity, echoes sound across the voice lines of Ex.29 which, although the ear may perceive, are not so apparent to the eye. From an opening interval of a perfect 5th, the first phrase sets a pattern which the forth-coming entries take up and imitate. In bar 4 another voice enters on E and follows the foregoing phrase in imitation but from an octave below (indicated by the second, overlapping phrase mark). At the end of this passage a third voice enters recalling the earlier entries but from an opening leap of a 4th. From a deeper register still the fourth voice enters in imitation on the low bass E.

Returning to the upper line, the passage from bar 5 (under the dotted curve) is also imitated at lower levels. Beginning on F sharp its five-note pattern is recalled in bar 9 but now from a 5th lower on B; and again from bar 13 on F sharp. The sheer symmetry of this design, with a minimum of notes, makes it a model of balance and brevity.

Unisons, octaves, 4ths and 5ths were the standard intervals in European music before 3rds and 6ths supplanted them. In the mediaeval chant 'organum', the voice parts are set almost exclusively in combinations of these intervals (Ex.30).

Ex. 30 Perfect intervals

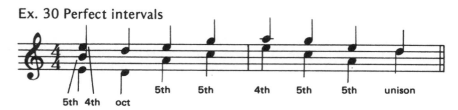

Debussy, Grieg and 20th century composers, attracted by the stark, almost archaic quality of perfect intervals have utilised them to evoke quasi-organum, oriental or pastoral strains in their music. The flavour of early music is captured, yet in a presentation essentially modern.

Perfect intervals merit investigation as refreshing alternatives to 3rds and 6ths for instrumental composition or song accompaniments. At a later stage chords will be constructed from 4ths and 5ths, but for the present the following exercises are a good introduction to them. With a melodic rather than a harmonic emphasis, they can be played in fast succession along the 2nd and 3rd strings, with or without syncopated open-string bass notes (Ex.31).

Ex. 31 Improvisations on the Dorian

Place the first and third left hand fingers on the 3rd and 2nd strings respectively as (a) at the beginning of Ex.31. This shape can be shifted to different fret positions as (b) and syncopated with open-bass strings E, A, D, and occasionally played against the open treble string E (c). To extend the range of 4ths, others may be played on the 2nd and 1st strings (d).

Consecutive perfect 4ths are ideal as accompanying lines for pentatonic tunes (provided that they are limited to the notes of the scale); or modal melodies such as Ex.32 which in this case is based on the Dorian mode.

Ex. 32 Doriana

Perfect and imperfect consonances

Some consonant intervals are more harmonious than others. Perfect consonances, as already stated, are unisons octaves and the 4ths and 5ths given. The other consonances, major/minor 3rds and 6ths, are slightly less balanced. Therefore these are categorised *imperfect* consonances. Both types are nevertheless passive intervals: they are more or less at rest. Linked to them, or conflicting with each other, are the forthcoming active note combinations or *dissonances*.

Dissonances: major/minor 2nds and 7ths; augmented 4ths and diminished 5ths

From mildy disgruntled to downright pungent, dissonances vary as much in levels of vibrancy as consonances do in shades of composure. Dissonances enliven an otherwise languid harmonic flow, they sharpen rhythms, they intensify expectancy. And yet they are elusive sounds, defying clear-cut description. Their degrees of potency can be assessed by direct comparison but that gives little indication of the potential energy that each one possesses. The strength of their impact depends as much on their surroundings as the state of conflict of their notes. In a predominantly consonant harmony a single dissonance will stand out; that same interval may dim in a whirl of other astringent sounds.

Context aside, when dissonances are compared, major and minor 2nds are the sharpest. Close behind are 7ths, and comparatively mild though still disruptive, are two intervals yet to be introduced: the augmented 4th and diminished 5th.

Major and minor 2nds

Until the second half of the 19th century, it was customary to follow a dissonance with a consonance. The clash of the dissonance would then be allayed or *resolved* by the repose of the consonance. Generally, the resolving consonance is an imperfect interval, a 3rd or 6th, though it can be an octave. Perfect 4ths and 5ths, those 'pure' but stark sounding intervals, are not the most effective resolving consonances. Major 2nds and less intense minor 2nds are resolved by one or both of their notes being replaced by those of a consonance (Exs.33).

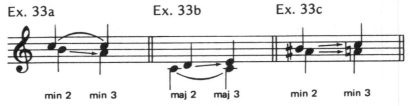

The 2nds in Exs.33a-b are resolved by *oblique motion:* one voice is held while the other rises or falls to complete a consonance. Ex.33c is the most decisive resolution of the three. In this the dissonance is resolved by *contrary motion:* where the parts move in opposite directions.

Ex. 34 Sonatine
Allegro moderato

Mauro Giuliani

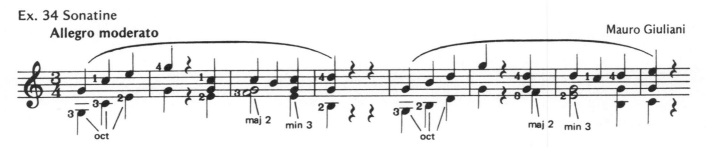

Concentrating on the resolution of the major 2nds, the first of these (bar 3) is particularly noticeable in that it falls on an accented beat. It is then resolved by the downward step of the bass line to a minor 3rd. The next major 2nd carries less impact, falling on a weak beat (the third beat in bar 6). Notice that its resolution gives rise to another dissonance, the minor 7th E-D. This interval, the next for discussion, is resolved by the descending step in the melody to a minor 6th E-C.

Major and minor 7ths

Intervals of 7ths occur more in vertical chord structures than as divisions in con-current melody lines. Major 7ths brighten common chords (Ex.35a), while minor 7ths disrupt them (Ex.35b).

Ex. 35a Resolution of major 7ths   Ex. 35b Resolution of minor 7ths

A chord containing a major 7th wavers somewhat but still retains its composure. In modern harmony, chords with major 7ths are often left un-resolved but if they are, their resolution could be to 6ths as Ex.35a. Chords containing minor 7ths are disgruntled and call for resolution. Both minor 7ths in Ex.35b are resolved by step in the melodies (B flat-A, C-B), and by leap in the bass lines (C-F, D-G).

Augmented 4ths and diminished 5ths

As well as consonant 4ths and 5ths, there are other 4ths and 5ths which are dissonant. These are *augmented 4ths* and *diminished 5ths*. An augmented 4th is three tones, a semitone wider than a perfect 4th. If, as in Ex.36a, a perfect 4th is 'stretched' by a semitone, its consonance will be distorted into a mournful dissonance.

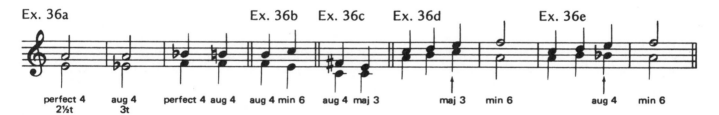

The augmented 4th in Ex.36b is resolved by contrary motion to a minor 6th: the top line is urged upwards, and the lower line gravitates downwards. In Ex.36c the augmented 4th is resolved by oblique motion: the lower note stays put while the upper line steps down to form a consonance. Exs.36d-e have the same upper lines, but Ex.36e, with an augmented 4th resolved by contrary motion, has a more decisive ending. A point to bear in mind, for if the option is open, and augmented 4th can be slipped into the end of a phrase to draw the parts to a snap conclusion.

Like the augmented 4th, a *diminished 5th* is three tones. When, as in Ex.37a, a perfect 5th is 'compressed' by a semitone, its consonance will change to dissonance. Ex.37b shows the resolution of a diminished 5th, and Exs.37c-d have the same upper lines with different subordinate parts: the latter, the stronger of the two, has a diminished 5th resolved by contrary motion.

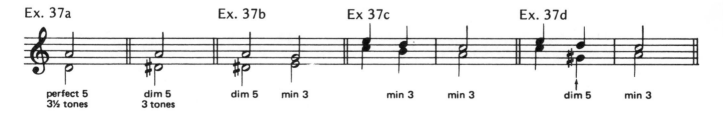

Two points of interest relating to the diminished 5th, the first pertaining to the Locrian mode omitted from Chapter One: B, C, D, E, F, G, A, B'. In this scale the 1st and 5th notes (tonic and dominant) are a diminished 5th, B-F. As these notes conflict rather than harmonise, the Locrian has been rejected as a basis for melodic composition (except in a few modern works). Secondly, the diminished 5th and its counterpart the augmented 4th being three-tones, are sometimes referred to as a *tritone*. Because of their dissonance, composers in mediaeval times nicknamed them the 'Devil's intervals'. What indeed would they have called some of the intervals that will turn up before this chapter is through?

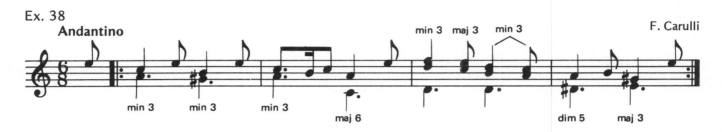

Ex. 38
Andantino
F. Carulli

Like 'Müss Ich denn', the upper line in Ex.38 is projected by underlying 3rds placed at accented beats. On reaching its highest point in the middle of the phrase, the melody begins a stepwise descent while the bass gradually rises to meet it. In the last bar a mild but mobile diminished 5th urges the phrase forward to its resolution, and a neatly timed ending on a major 3rd.

Augmented 2nds, 6ths and octaves; diminished 3rds, 7ths and octaves

Intervals other than 4ths and 5ths are sometimes augmented and diminished. If the upper note of a major 2nd is raised it will become an augmented 2nd (Ex.39a).

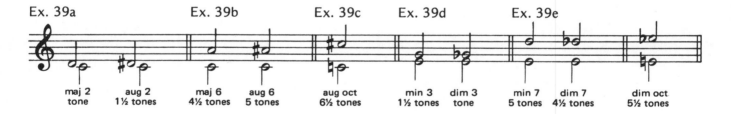

As the upper note D sharp of the augmented 2nd in Ex.39a is also E flat, then why not notate that interval as a minor 3rd, C-E flat? One instance where sharps are preferred to flats is in ascending melody lines — where sharps imply ascent. Another reason for notating D sharp as distinct from E flat is to conform with a musical notation that includes other sharp notes. The grammar of the music is then kept consistent.

For the same reasons, 6ths may be augmented as Ex.39b (instead of a minor 7th C-B flat); and octaves augmented as Ex.39c (instead of a minor 9th C-D flat). If the upper note of a minor 3rd is lowered as Ex.39d, the interval is diminished; and if the upper note of a minor 7th or octave is lowered, they too are classified diminished (Ex.39e).

Interval inversions

When the lower note of an interval is removed and placed an octave higher, the interval is *inverted* (Ex.40).

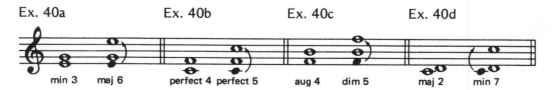

An inverted minor 3rd is a major 6th (Ex40a); an inverted perfect 4th is a perfect 5th (Ex.40b); an inverted augmented 4th is a diminished 5th (Ex.40c); and an inverted major 2nd is a minor 7th (Ex.40d). Conversely, if the major 6th in Ex.40a was inverted it would revert to the minor 3rd shown. Similarly for the other intervals: invert a minor 7th and a major 2nd results.

These inversions reveal some interesting points. When 3rds or 6ths are inverted their numerical size is halved or doubled as the case may be, but they remain imperfect, and as such, blend well. Similiarly, when perfect 4ths and 5ths are inverted they remain perfect, reflecting each other's distinctive starkness. An inverted tritone remains a tritone — bearing in mind that an augmented 4th is the same size as a diminished 5th. Inverted major 2nds and 7ths also retain their dissonance as minor 7ths and 2nds.

In short, when major intervals are inverted they become minor; when perfect intervals are inverted, they remain perfect. When augmented intervals are inverted, they become diminished. As to the change of numerical size, think of the number nine as the key. To invert a 7th, subtract 7 from 9 which leaves 2 or a 2nd; to invert a 6th, subtract 6 from 9 leaving 3 or a 3rd. To invert a 4th, subtract 4 from 9 and then see.

Dissonance in 20th century music

In most formal contemporary music, dissonance enjoys complete freedom. The traditional fetters that once controlled it — judicious use, and obligatory resolution — have long since been discarded. Since the second half of the 19th century, composers have extended their vocabularies with increasing dissonance. In the early years of the 20th century, those composers in the vanguard of modern music introduced new idioms steeped in dissonance. Epitomised in the progressive works of Arnold Schoenberg (1874-1951), and Igor Stravinsky (1882-1971), these highly-charged musical idioms precipitated what now amounts to the liberation of dissonance.

Not that consonance is regarded as a spent force. Far from it, many of today's composers seek to balance consonance with dissonance. It is just that resolution of dissonance in the old way is no longer considered requisite. Even so, resolution of a kind does take place in a predominately dissonant harmony through the alternation of pungent with less emphatic dissonance. This fluctuation of tension may be sustained on a taut level, but it can offer as much variety as exchanges of consonance and dissonance.

In differing degrees of tension, some of these intervals are given in Exs.41. Isolated and in the raw they may jar somewhat. In the examples that follow, that effect will be both cushioned and projected in full. For the present they represent a mere sample from this vital area of sound. But it is important to introduce them here not only to show the vibrant end of the interval spectrum but because they are primary musical elements of our day and age.

Ex. 41a   Ex. 41b

min 2   aug oct   maj 2   maj 9   min 2   aug oct   min 2   aug oct   maj 7   tri   maj 7   tri

Arranged horizontally as melodic intervals, and then vertically as segments of chords, the most acute dissonances are the minor 2nds and altered octaves (Ex.41a). These and major 2nds have an edge over the major 7ths and tritones in Ex.41b.

In the first of three examples utilising these intervals, Ex.42 has the rhythm of its already vivacious melody accentuated by major 2nds struck on the first and third beats.

Ex. 42 No.2 from Four Pieces

Vivo

Jean Absil

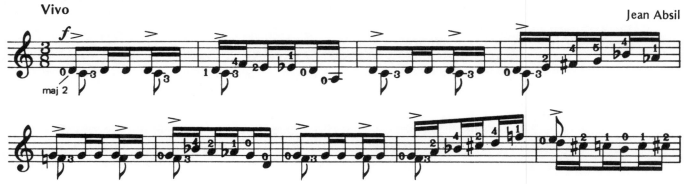

From the punctuated dissonances in this excerpt, we move on to another example, again with two voice parts but more angular in shape and clashing in virtually unrelenting dissonances (Ex.43).

Ex. 43 Miniature No.9

Slowly

L.B.

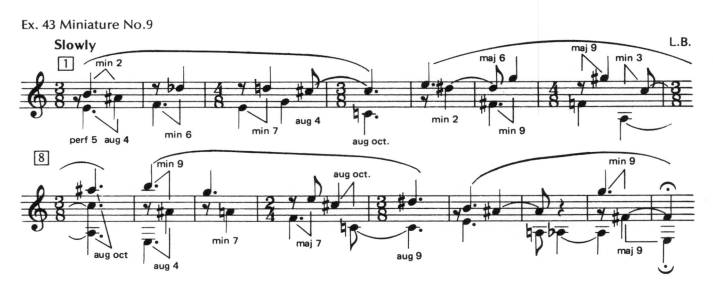

Despite the slow tempo constraining the lines of Ex.43, their dissonant and erratic leaps urges them forward without respite. Most prominent are the altered octaves or 'false relations' resulting from conflicts between the two voice parts. And yet for all their agitation, the lines are contained within a symmetrical framework of four balanced phrases. The first phrase starts with a minor 2nd, B-A sharp, and ends with an altered octave, bar 4. This is balanced by the response of the second phrase, also beginning with a minor 2nd (bar 5) and ending with an altered octave (bar 8). The beginning of the third phrase, the melody's peak, is accentuated by a minor 9th, an augmented 4th and a stark perfect 5th, E-B. Notice also that these intervals recall the notes in bar 1, but they are now spread by octave displacement. This phrase, like the two before, ends restlessly but does suggest by its ascent to D sharp (bar 12) that E will follow, hence the return of the bass in bar 1. Gradually working round to settle on this tonal centre, the fourth phrase falls a step to A sharp, and this semitone is echoed in the bass descent, A-A flat. Echoes continue but distantly through minor and major 9th inversions, G-F sharp, F sharp-E, where the latter step falls to the tonal note on which the bass began and now rests.

Ex. 44 Reflections

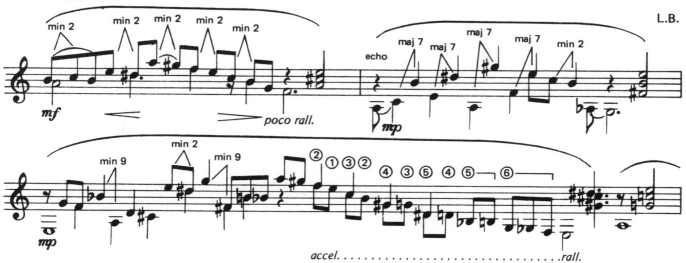

L.B.

What appears to be mainly a melodic array of 2nds and 7ths is not quite the case, for they are heard harmonically too. One note, often that produced by an open string, continues to sound while the next note, a 2nd or 7th away, overlaps. Consequently, the dissonances are sustained for longer than the melodic steps and leaps suggest in the notation. The 'echo' indicated at the beginning of the second phrase is conveyed in two ways: through the change of dynamics from mezzo forte (moderately loud), to mezzo piano (moderately soft); and by invoking intervals from the first phrase and inverting them in the next. While the opening phrase ascends in 2nds A-B, B-C, C-B, these intervals are inverted in the second phrase as major 7ths. 2nds and 7ths are continued through into the third phrase, and are then aligned as a fluid descent of open and stopped-string dissonances to complete the section.

Selecting examples in which particular consonances and dissonances predominated made it possible to evaluate their qualities and effects more or less individually. To conclude, a melody will be harmonised with a counter line in three distinctive styles. On its own that melody is nondescript, but given a supporting line it takes on a definite identity. As three contrasting possibilities, the upper line in Ex.45 is harmonised first with 3rds and 6ths plus one resolved dissonance as it might be for a folk song or popular instrumental arrangement; then with perfect 4ths and 5ths to give it an exotic, archaic-like flavour; and finally in total dissonance with an astringent and progressive character.

Ex. 45 Imperfect consonances   Perfect consonances   Dissonances

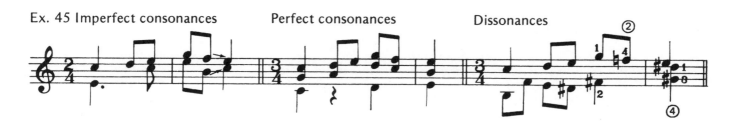

The same melody in three different guises undergoes a complete change of character on each appearance. The first is relaxed, the second stark, the third taut. Three distinctive types of intervals, the building blocks for chords and their progressions.

3: BASIC CHORD PROGRESSIONS

Setting the chords to a melody is certainly an interesting undertaking; but you may have discovered, that is not without problems. Not only must the chords provide a background for the melody, they must also fit together in a way that enhances its gestures, its rise and fall, its pauses and rests. If the melody is unconventional and modern in style, your imagination has a fairly free rein since its chords and counter lines need not comply with traditional patterns and frameworks. Vintage lines, on the other hand, usually call for accompaniments befitting their style. Their chord progressions tend to follow established sequences; and although these may not offer as much scope for novelty, they can be modified and embellished to suit any number of different songs.

Besides laying guidelines for song accompaniments, a knowledge of basic chord progressions has many other advantages. Most simple pieces from the classical repertoire are structured from them. A measure of common chords leads to an understanding of the melodic and harmonic construction of these compositions. Blues and popular instrumental solos too, stripped of their idiomatic ornamentation, often draw upon standard chords set in familiar progressions.

Before chord progressions can be outlined, there are the chords themselves to consider: what intervals they comprise, how those intervals are assembled, and the part that they play in the overall sound of the chords. While there are dozens of chords in everyday use, there are just a few basic types. These in turn can be narrowed down to three-note kernels called *triads*.

Ex. 46 C major triad

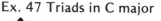

The triad in Ex.46 has the three fundamental notes of the chord C major (abbreviated Cmaj. or simply C). Its notes are first placed vertically, in which case they would be sounded together, and are then staggered to illustrate their interval layout. From the lowest note or *root*, the triad receives its letter name. The *middle* note E is a major 3rd above the root, and the *upper* note G is a perfect 5th above the root.

For several centuries, triads in different forms were the principal chordal units in Western harmony. Though they no longer monopolise, they continue as the staple chords in folk song accompaniments, popular music arrangements, and are far from obsolete in formal contemporary harmony. Appearing in all shapes and sizes, their notes may be tightly grouped or spread out by octave duplication to form four, five and six-note chords.

In the same way that Ex.46 was constructed on the tonic of the scale, a complete range of triads can be built by superimposing 3rds on other scale degrees. Derived from that scale, those triads will be closely associated with it. However, a composition based on the scale C major has not sole claim to them for they are also harmonic constituents of other scale foundations. But within C major they are paired into recognised progressions. After examining the construction of each triad built on and with the notes of C major, chord progressions closely associated with this scale will then be set from its range of triad chords.

Ex. 47 Triads in C major

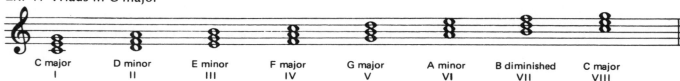

Just as the tonic triad received its letter name from its root C, the triads in Ex.47 are letter named according to their respective roots: Dminor — D, F, A; Eminor — E, G, B. Roman numerals are used for chord numbers to avoid confusion when other figures are included to indicate added and altered notes in the chords.*

* To distinguish chord from scale names in the present text, chords are denoted as Cmajor, etc., and scales as C major.

Classifying triads: major, minor and diminished

When the lower interval of a triad is a major 3rd, and its upper interval is a minor 3rd, that triad is classified *major* (Ex.48a).

Ex. 48a major triads

Conversely, when the lower interval is a minor 3rd and the upper a major 3rd, the triad is *minor* (abbreviated Dmin or Dm, Ex.48b). Whether major or minor, the outer interval of the triad is a perfect 5th.

Ex. 48b minor triads

Classifying triads major or minor is not just to distinguish between their interval layouts. Major triads reflect their lower major 3rds with a prominent 'major' sounding quality. Minor triads with their lower minor 3rds, sound contrastingly subdued or 'minor'. Both types are nevertheless *concords:* they comprise only consonant intervals (Ex.49).

Ex. 49

The odd man out is the chord on the VII degree. With lower and upper intervals of a minor 3rd, its outer interval is a diminished 5th: hence its classification, *diminished* (abbreviated Bdim or B°, Ex.49). Because it has a dissonant interval, B diminished lacks the composure of a major and minor chord. A restless, unstable triad it is a *discord.*

In their present compressed state, the difference between the triads' major, minor and diminished sound qualities is not clearly distinguishable. But when their notes are spread out through octave displacement, they can then be compared as practical chords (Ex.50).

Ex. 50 Chords in C major

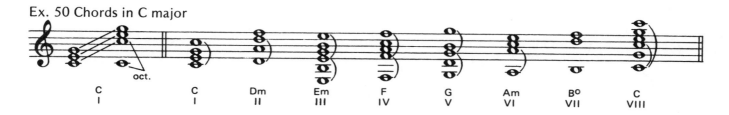

Each triad has now developed into a fully-fledged guitar chord. Rearranging their notes and supplementing them with octaves has increased the density and size of the chords without undermining their individual sound qualities. Notice that the root's octave is present in every chord except Bdiminished. This is the best note of the three to double since its octave emphasises the root as the fundamental of the chord. The 5th may also be doubled, but the 3rd only rarely. A 3rd with its octave tends to overpower the root, rendering the chord weak and 'tinny' in sound. On the rare occasions when the 3rd and its octave are present in a chord, the two are not generally played together but one after the other, and even then, with intervening notes (Ex.51).

Ex. 51 Study in C major

F. Sor

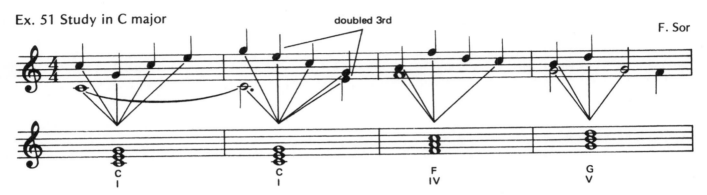

When enlarging a triad, any of its notes can be uppermost. For instance, from the chord Cmajor either C, E or G can be placed in the upper melody line. The note assigned to the melody has a direct bearing on the sound of the chord, for being the highest note, it is the most prominent. In the second bar of Ex.51 Cmajor has as its highest note G. Now this particular formation sounds different from another arrangement of the same chord with C on top. Nevertheless, the two chords have the same *characteristic* sound: they are both basically *major* triads with a *root C.*

Omitted notes

To facilitate left hand fingering, or for the sake of clarity, one of the fundamental notes of a triad may be omitted even though others in it are doubled. In major and minor chords the omitted note is likely to be the 5th, since the absence of this is the least noticeable of the three, e.g. Cmajor — C, E, G, omit G. Except in complex chord structures, the root and 3rd are not omitted as their loss obscures the chords' major/minor qualities.

Chord progressions

For all their individuality, most simple guitar studies, and many advanced ones too, have much in common. They generally embody just three or four basic chords, and these tend to follow stock progressions. Folk song accompaniments also revolve around a few chords, and they too trace the same harmonic routes as those of instrumental studies. Usually three chords associated with the scale on which the music is based take precedence in that they function as the harmony's superstructure. Called the *primary* chords, they are built on the 1st, 4th and 5th degrees of the major scale (Ex.52).

Ex. 52 Primary chords in C major

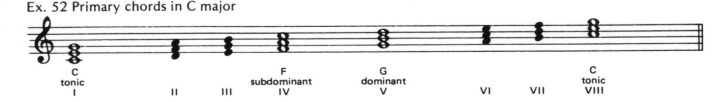

The most important chord of the group is I or the *tonic*. This is the king-pin, and like the tonic note in a melody, the tonic chord in a progression usually marks the beginning and end of the harmony, and acts as a crossing or resting point during its journey. The next most important chord is V or the *dominant*. The mutual attraction of the tonic and dominant in a melody extends to the tonic and dominant chords in a progression. So naturally are the tonic and dominant chords inclined to each other that the harmony of many folk songs and instrumental pieces is often no more than a reciprocation of these two chords. Occasionally IV or the *subdominant* is called upon to bridge the tonic to the dominant (Ex.53a); alternatively it may direct the harmony back to the tonic (Ex.53b).

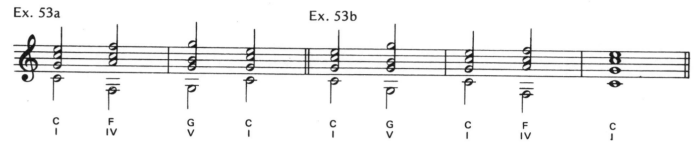

Depending on their order, the primary chords will either steer the harmony outwards from the tonic chord where it can then pause and take stock; or draw it gently or forcefully back to the tonic to temporary or permanent rest. To see which combination gives rise to these effects, the primary chords will be linked not into a continuous progression, but paired as *cadences*.

Cadences in C major

Cadences define the structural divisions in the harmony, the beginning, the ending and the pause of a phrase. One cadence will suspend a phrase in mid-course, another will draw it gracefully to rest, and another still will urge it to a temporary or permanent conclusion. Of the three primary chord cadences, the most decisive is the *full close* or *perfect cadence*. This is the dominant to tonic chords, V-I (Ex.54a).

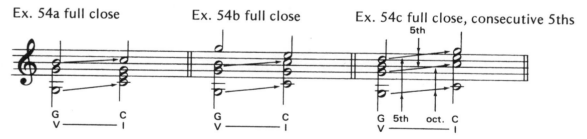

A full close draws the harmony home to its tonic chord. This may take place at intermediate stages of a progression, but it is most effective for its conclusion. This cadence is the most decisive primary chord progression for two reasons: first, its bass notes (dominant to tonic, G-C) are mutually attracted; and secondly, the leading-note (B) in the dominant chord is compelled to rise via a semitone to the upper tonic (C) in the tonic chord.

With its upper line ending on the tonic note, Ex.54a is the most resolute cadence of the three. Less conclusive, the upper line of Ex.54b ends with the 3rd of the tonic chord. Least convincing is the full close in Ex.54c. Its consecutive octaves and 5ths pervade and consequently dilute the harmony with their stark sounding quality. For this reason consecutive octaves and 5ths are avoided in conventional harmony. In practice, however, these do occur, and not least in guitar music. Given the limitations of the fretboard, it is sometimes physically impracticable to follow the 'rules' regarding the avoidance of parallel 5ths and octaves in guitar chord progressions.

Ex. 55 Foggy dew. C major

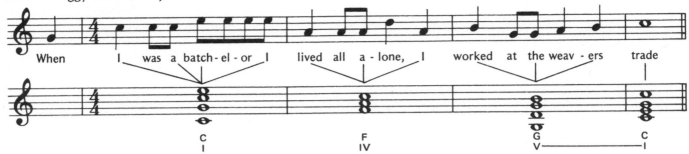

When I was a batch-el-or I lived all a-lone, I worked at the weav-ers trade

C   F   G   C
I   IV   V————I

Before the chords behind Ex.55 or a similar melody can be deduced, the scale on which the line is based must first be determined. Its initial upbeat leap of a 4th, G-C, suggests C major, and a glance along the melody notes, also from C major, particularly their last semitone step, confirms this. As the basis of the melody is C major, then the accompanying chords will be built on and with those notes. And considering the simplicity of the line, it is likely that primary chords only will suffice.

A fair but not explicit indication of how the accompaniment might go can be deduced by visually sorting out pertinent melody notes. The first bar or so is examined to see which notes are accented, or take priority by virtue of their duration. These notes may need a separate chord to support them, or, as is more often the case, one chord will support a span of them. Seeing as the first accented note in the first full bar of Ex.55 is C, and the other melody notes in that bar (C and E) are contained in the triad Cmajor, then this chord will start the ball rolling. Another reason for choosing the tonic as the first chord is that it will emphasise from the outset the tonic note of the melody and harmony. Moving to the next bar or span of the melody, the same procedure is adopted: important notes are singled out and duplicated in the supporting chord. For this bar, Fmajor both accommodates the repeated melody note A, and acts as a bridge to the next chord Gmajor, suggested by G and B in that bar of the melody. Ending the progression with a full close both emphasises the return of the tonic in the melody, and draws the harmony to rest on its central chord.

This accompaniment can be seen as a progression of chords where each chord supports the span of melody notes arching above it. Guitar instrumental pieces are often conceived in a different way; their melodies fringe their chords or are laced into them, and sometimes underpin them as prominent bass lines. As often as not, an instrumental work is composed by the reverse process to that just described: instead of a chord progression devised for a given melody, a melody is gleaned from a known chord progression. The opening of the melody is derived from notes in the first chord, followed through with notes from the second, and continues to unfold from a predetermined chord progression (Ex.56).

Ex. 56 Study in C

C   C   F   C   C   F   G   C
I   I   IV   I   I   IV   V————I

Offering few surprises, Ex.56 probably grew from its stock progression of primary chords. Here the chord notes are sustained and rhythmically motivated, played in 'harp-like' fashion or as *arpeggios*. Between the arpeggiated notes are others marked by asterisks which are not actually component or *essential* notes of the chords. As *unessential* or *passing* notes, they are inset to improve the continuity of the lines.

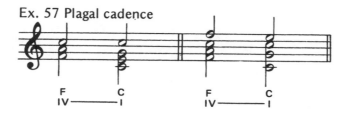

Ex. 57 Plagal cadence

Like the full close, a plagal cadence also centres the harmony on the tonic chord. Unlike a full close, however, which imparts a considerable driving force, a plagal cadence is a more gentle chord change. Frequently ending passages of hymns, a plagal cadence is sometimes called an *Amen cadence* (see also Ex.81).

The last primary chord cadence is the *half close* or *imperfect cadence*, usually the tonic to dominant or subdominant to dominant. As its name suggests, a half close grants the harmonic flow respite, allowing it to gather breath, as it were, on the dominant chord (Ex.58).

Ex. 58 Half close cadence

Ex. 59 Sonata in C, opus 81

F. Carulli

Larghetto

From its tonic chord Ex.59 divides into two voice parts moving by contrary motion. Notice how the bass line's descent from F to C in bar 1 is imitated by the descending upper line in bar 2. Though both parts pause on the dominant chord at a half close, they convey a further sense of movement. In this case the melody remains centred on the dominant chord into bar 3. To balance the foregoing imitation is another over bars 3 and 4. Here the bass line descends from G to D, and its imitation, the upper line in bar 4, is carried through to the tonic C.

Key and keynote

On the tonic chord the harmony rests. Around its tonic note the melody revolves. This note, the anchor for the melody and harmony, is called its *keynote*. Those melodies shown have encircled their keynote, intersected it during their course, and ended on it. The keynote is also the root of the tonic chord, the harmony's point of departure and return. As it happens, all the recent examples are centred on a common keynote, the note C. Because those melodies and chords were constructed mainly with notes from the scale of C major, they are based on that scale or are in the *key of C major*. This does not mean that a composition in the key of C major is restricted solely to the notes of that scale; but provided that C major, or whatever the key may be, is initially established by the melody and harmony, and that they ultimately centre upon it, the sense of a specific key will prevail.

In their different ways, primary chord cadences endorse the status of the keynote: the decisive fall to the tonic in a full close; the lapse of a plagal cadence; and the poise of the half close on the dominant. In and around these harmonic mainstays, further resources can be drawn into play; they are the *secondary* chords in the key built on II, III, VI and VII degrees of the scale (Ex.60).

Ex. 60 Secondary chords in C major

Apart from where the melody specifically calls for the support of the primary chords, it usually allows for alternative harmonisations. Often melodic subdivisions have notes that are common to two or three chords. When those chords are known the harmony can be varied by substituting one chord for another or combining them. Looking to the secondary chords we can see what optional harmonisations are available. Each secondary chord in Ex.60 will be partnered with, and will sometimes substitute, one of the primary chords. For example, II the supertonic can often be interchanged with the subdominant as these chords have two notes in common: Dminor — D, F, A; Fmajor — F, A, C. Similarly, VI the submediant shares two notes with the tonic chord: Aminor — A, C, E; Cmajor — C, E, G. Melody permitting, these minor chords may be linked with or substitute their respective majors.

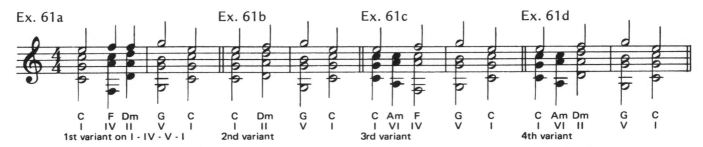

Keeping pretty much to the same melody, Exs.61 are variants of the primary chord progression I-IV-V-I. If this progression happens to be the accompaniment for a folk song or the principal harmony for a prospective instrumental work, its variants will be refreshing alternatives. Ex.61a has Dminor substituting Fmajor for the last beat of the first bar; in Ex.61b, Dminor substitutes Fmajor completely, lending a marked minor shade to what was an all-major harmony. Ex.61c has VI replacing the tonic chord for the second beat of the first bar; and Ex.61d enlists both secondary chords as an elaboration of the original primary chord progression.

Homophony and counterpoint

When, as in Exs.61, the chord notes are given a vertical emphasis in that they serve mainly as harmonic supports for single melody notes or overhead spans of them, the setting is *homophonic*. With a horizontal emphasis, the chord notes may be arranged as two or more interdependent melodies running simultaneously in *counterpoint* (Ex.62).

Ex. 62 Study in C   M. Carcassi

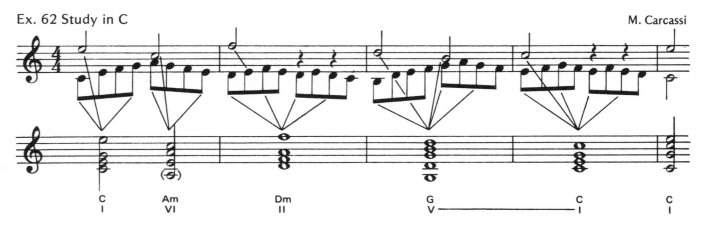

Guided by the chord progression shown in Ex.61d this simple contrapuntal piece has two more or less independent parts of contrasting natures: an upper sparsely set melody over an active bass line. In this instance each part can be heard clearly enough, but there is of course a limit to the number of voice parts that can be maintained simultaneously within the range of the guitar fretboard. However, as the next study shows both in notation and its pictorial illustration, three parts progress without confinement or loss of separation (Ex.63)

Ex. 63 Study in C

F. Sor

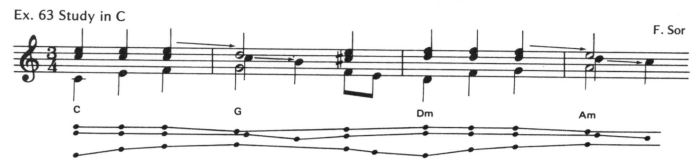

Like all contrapuntal settings, Ex.63 strikes a balance between the horizontal layout of its voice parts, and the vertical progression of its chords. Those chords may either derive from the lines or be the guiding force behind them. Whichever the case, they will progress in what the composer considers to be a logical order. From one of Fernando Sor's finest studies, Ex.63 has three horizontal lines bound up with four principal chords: two majors on one side contrasted with two minors on the other. The most active voice part is the bass line, which in its initial ascent spans a 5th, C-G. At the end of this ascent, the upper line falls a tone, and behind that, the centre line falls a semitone, C-B. To balance and contrast this statement, the next two bars respond with minor chords. Following the same patterns set by the foregoing voices, the two upper lines in this section of the phrase also descend a step, and the bass ascends a corresponding 5th, D-A.

Of the two remaining secondary chords, III the mediant sounds strangely out of place in a C major surrounding, and VII the leading-note chord, a discord, requires resolution. With these potentially alien qualities, it is necessary to bolster III and VII with staunch primary harmonies. III may be partnered with the tonic by virtue of their common notes (Eminor — E, G, B; Cmajor — C, E, G); and VII may be partnered with or substitute the dominant (Bdiminished — B, D, F; Gmajor — G, B, D).

Ex. 64a   Ex. 64b   Ex. 64c

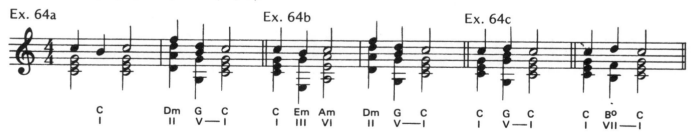

Ex.64a is a four-beat bar with a Cmajor harmony followed by the supertonic and a full close. Ex.64b, an embellishment of this progression, has III and VI taking three beats originally held by Cmajor.

If the opportunity arises whereby the leading-note chord can be favoured over the dominant, the resolution of a VII-I progression is a pleasant change to the overworked full close. In Ex.64c the melody note D is harmonised with Gmajor, and then as suggested, with Bdiminished (see also Ex.65).

Ex. 65 Study in C major

Giuliani

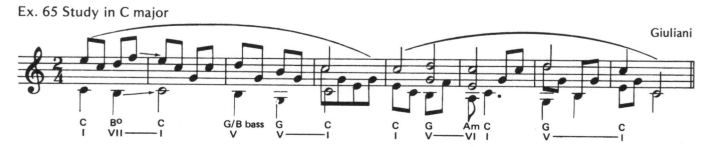

No sooner do the lines in Ex.65 depart from their tonic chord than pivot back to it through Bdiminished. With its bass leading-note B rising, and upper line falling in contrary motion, this progression is almost as resolute as the full close at the end of the phrase. In the second phrase the melodic interest is at first given to the bass which falls to A, the root of VI in an *interrupted* or *deceptive* cadence. Instead of the anticipated tonic, VI follows the dominant, and in so doing, diverts the harmony from a full close. A pictorial representation of the chord progression for this piece is shown in Ex.66.

Ex. 66

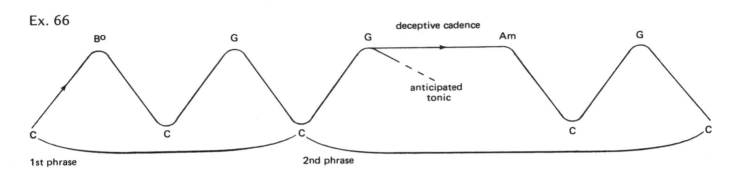

1st phrase   2nd phrase

Deceptive rather than interrupted is a more fitting term for this cadence; it doesn't so much interrupt the harmonic flow as divert it evasively from its expected return to the tonic. And most effective it is too, particularly for prolonging the last verse of a song or the final line of an instrumental work. In place of a full close at the end of a progression, the deceptive cadence will permit either the preceding phrase or verse to be repeated, or act as a springboard for a last-moment instrumental flourish.

Thinking back to the group of triads first shown, its compact three-note chords gave little indication then of their potential for such a wide variety of melodic and harmonic patterns. The first stage of their development was the expansion of primary triads into four, five and six-note chord formations. Paired as cadences, the primary chords drew the harmony to rest on the dominant, and directed it forcefully or gently back home to the tonic. Then came the secondary chords, dovetailed between or taking the place of the primary chords in the key. Though there are no hard and fast rules governing the use of these, secondary chords merge naturally with those primary chords with which they have notes in common.

Whether the chord notes were spread as arpeggios, played together as block chords or strung into two or more horizontal melodies, they had as their foundation the scale C major with its keynote C. The next move is to transfer this scale and its harmony to higher or lower levels through a process called *transposition.*

4: TRANSPOSITION

In recalling a line from a song, a pattern of notes come to mind retracing the melodic steps and leaps left by the earlier impression. Yet however closely that later rendition may seem to tally with the former one, it call still differ in one important respect: the notes chosen to imitate the melody will be those that fall within easy range of the voice — not necessarily the exact ones heard in the first instance. If, for its repeat, the notes of the melody are shifted from their original tonal range, and are sung at another level where they are easier to pitch, the singer has *transposed* the tune.

As well as vocal lines, instrumental melodies often require transposing. A work written for, say, the cello may need to be transposed before it can be played on the guitar. In some keys, instrumental melodies can be harmonised with ease; in others their chords are inaccessible. If the harmony cannot be added conveniently to the line in its existing key, its transposition to another key, hence to a different position on the fretboard, could place its chords within reach.

Transposition entails not just shifting an awkward passage here and there, but transferring the entire composition to a different tonal range. To illustrate the steps taken in this procedure, a simple tune will be transposed from the key of C major up to G major. Following this are transpositions of modal melodies, chord progressions and a phrase from an instrumental piece.

Ex. 67 Eriskay C major

While the melody in Ex.67 is not difficult to play, the low bass notes in its third and fourth phrases may present vocal hurdles. But if these notes only were raised, that would distort the tune's overall shape. So the line must be shifted in its entirety to a higher level. Here then is the same melody transposed up five steps or a 5th higher (Ex.68).

Ex. 68 Eriskay 2nd rendition

Where the earlier version began with C, this one, a 5th higher, begins with G. And as all its other notes are relatively higher too, those once awkward passages are now within easy vocal range.

Returning to the former melody, that is clearly in the key of C major. Its first three notes are those of the tonic triad, its very last note is C, and the notes between are from the scale of C major. To assist the forthcoming transposition of this scale, its tone-semitone order is reviewed in Ex.69.

Ex. 69 C major

1 t 2 t 3 st 4 t 5 t 6 t 7 st 8

As the tonic C of the scale C major is also the first note of the initial melody, it follows that the scale for the transposition will have a tonic G — the first note of the second rendition. Having fixed the tonic for the latter scale, its other notes can be deduced by marking them out with the same tone-semitone order as in C major. If the order of tones and semitones from G does not match those in C major, the second melody would have been based on a different type of scale. It would then have emerged as a variation of the former melody, and not as it does, a duplication of it at another pitch level.

Ex. 70 G major

tonic t 2 t 3 st 4 t 5 t 6 t 7 st 8

In transposing the major scale to G major, it is necessary to sharpen the 7th degree so that G major, like C major, will have a semitone step preceding its upper tonic. As the tone-semitone order of the other notes conforms with the corresponding notes in C major, it is not necessary to alter these.

Looking once more at the G major version of 'Eriskay', this contains the raised 7th degree, F sharp in bar 5. From this to the next note G is an upward step of a semitone. This semitone corresponds with the semitone B-C at the same position in the C major melody. No other adjustments are necessary. Like their major scales, both melodies follow the same sequence of tones and semitones even though the latter is pitched at a higher level.

Key signatures

In the transposition of 'Eriskay' the sharp sign was entered directly against the pertinent note. In practice it is not usual to enter sharp signs in the notation whenever a 7th degree turns up as they would needlessly clutter the score. Instead, one sharp only is written at the beginning of the stave as a *key signature* (Ex.71).

Ex. 71 Key signature for G major

F sharp   F sharp   F sharp   F sharp

A key signature indicates which notes are to be sharpened (or flattened) consistently throughout a composition. With no sharps or flats, C major has no key signature; but G major does have one, a single sharp placed next to the treble clef on the upper line of the stave, Ex.71. This sharp sign not only applies to the F note nearest the clef, but to all F notes however high or low they may be.

Other popular major keys

In addition to C and G major, other popular major keys are D, A, E, F, B flat and E flat major. To conform to the major scale tone-semitone order those scales beginning with D, A and E must have certain degrees sharpened; whereas the scales beginning with F, B flat and E flat need flats. These scales are shown in Ex.72 with their sharp or flat signs entered in brackets against the notes to clarify their major scale tone-semitone layouts; and to the left of the scales are their key signatures.

Ex. 72

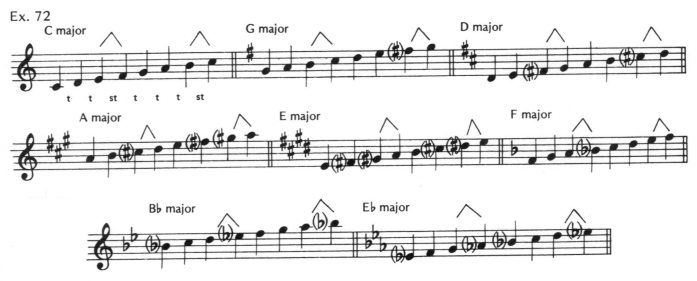

The most accessible major scales on the guitar are those which include notes produced by open strings. For example, the notes from the 2nd, 3rd, 4th and 5th open strings (B, G, D, A) are all contained in G major. Since these strings need only be struck by right hand fingers and not stopped by those of the left, physical problems are minimised. Therefore scales with open string notes are preferred as the bases for instrumental compositions, particularly those written for beginners.

Songs, as mentioned earlier, can be transposed to a key most suited to the singer's voice. Generally, though, the favoured keys for folk songs are C, G and D major. Popular blues keys are A and E major. Their open 5th and 6th strings are especially important as they, being keynotes, are frequently sounded throughout a blues accompaniment or instrumental solo. Major keys with flat notes are preferred for brass band arrangements or music where brass instruments predominate, the reason being that brass instruments are tuned to flat notes just as E, A and D are open string tunings on the guitar.

Naming a major scale from its key signature

If you see a key signature and cannot recall the name of its associated major scale, the following method will enable you to do so.

Ex. 73a

D major

Ex. 73b

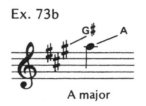

A major

Ex. 73c

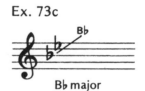

Bb major

To name a major scale with sharps in its key signature, count up a semitone from the outer sharp sign. The name of the note a semitone above this sharp sign is the same as the letter name for the associated major scale. In Ex.73a the outer sharp sign indicates C sharp. A semitone above this is D, the name of that key signature's major scale, D major. If there is only one sharp in the key signature (F sharp), count a semitone up from that: F sharp to G, or G major. In Ex.73b the outer sharp sign indicates G sharp. A semitone above G sharp is A, the name of the major scale, A major.

The name of a major scale with flats in its key signature is the same as the name of the last but one flat shown. Ex.73c has two flats, B flat and E flat in its key signature. The letter name for this major scale is the same as the penultimate note B flat in the key signature.

For reference, the following table shows the keynotes (the tonics) for popular major keys with their associated key signatures (Ex.74).

Ex. 74 Table of Key Signatures

Key Signature	𝄞	𝄞♯	𝄞♯♯	𝄞♯♯♯	𝄞♯♯♯♯	𝄞♭	𝄞♭♭	𝄞♭♭♭
Keynote (Starting note)	C	G	D	A	E	F	Bb	Eb

Modal scale transpositions

From singer to singer, region to region, folk song was disseminated by verbal exchange. Nursery rhymes, quaint or strangely morbid, songs of labour, of love and the wild oat, have passed through generations by word of mouth. Though a vast corpus of traditional folk songs has survived, many must inevitably have disappeared in the upsurge of modern music styles. Certainly more would have shared the same fate had it not been for devotees who sought to preserve their musical heritage in unadulterated form. The songs they gathered tell of work and leisure in industrial societies and of rural singers far removed from urban life. They are the songs that Cecil Sharp collected from ale houses in Somerset and settlers in the Southern Appalachians; the American folk songs and blues recorded by Alan Lomax; the extensive researches of Béla Bartók into Balkan folklore, and those of Maud Karpeles into English folk song.

The legacies from these and other collectors are available in published anthologies. Many are modal, and being notated exactly as sung, are often based on transpositions of the modal scales shown in Chapter One. Those have no sharps or flats but their transpositions do, and they are usually indicated by one of the key signatures shown earlier. Given such a song and wishing to harmonise it, it's useful, sometimes essential, to know what its underlying scale is. But then there is the problem of indentifying the mode with a key signature that is common to numerous other scales. The key signature does in fact point half way to the answer, and determining the keynote will complete it.

Ex. 75 The little Turtle Dove

At first glance the key signature of two sharps in Ex.75 suggests D major as the basis for the melody. Closer observation will show that this is not the scale as its two phrases come firmly to rest on the note B. Since D is not the keynote of the melody, nor D major its scale, consider next the possibility of a modal basis, bearing in mind the nature of the song. Knowing that it has a tonic B and a key signature of two sharps, the scale can be written out as Ex.76.

Comparing the tone-semitone order of this scale against those in Chapter One, it follows the Aeolian mode (Ex.77).

Ex. 77 Aeolian

Then the basis for 'Little Turtle Dove' is the Aeolian mode transposed to start on B, hence *B-Aeolian*.

Ex. 78 Cock Robin. E-Aeolian

'Who killed Cock Rob-in?'   'I' said the spar - row,   'with my bow and ar - row'
'Who saw him die?'   'I' said the fly,   'with my tee - ny eye'
'Who made his cof - fin?'   'I' said the snipe,   'with my pock- et knife'
'Who'll dig his grave?'   'I' said the crow,   'with my spade and hoe'

accomp.

The key signature in Ex.78 does not apply to G major because its first and third phrases end on E, the melody's keynote. So consider next a modal scale with a tonic E and one sharp, F sharp, its 2nd degree. Comparing this tone-semitone order with those in Chapter One, only one mode has a semitone step from its 2nd to 3rd, and 5th to 6th degrees, the Aeolian, in the case *E-Aeolian* (Ex.79).

Ex. 79 E-Aeolian

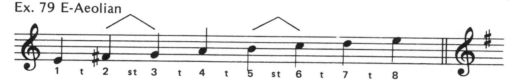

1 t 2 st 3 t 4 t 5 st 6 t 7 t 8

As a point of interest, this beautiful plaintive fable has, it seems, echoed through schoolrooms and across hearths for centuries. The Oxford Dictionary of Nursery Rhymes states that the earliest known version is c.1744, and points out that its origins are buried in antiquity. A variant of the last verse has 'owl' rhymed with 'shovel', suggesting that the 14th century *shouell* or *showl* for shovel was the correct reading.

'Who'll dig his grave'?

'I', said the Owl

'with my pick and shovel'.

The following reference table shows the key signatures and keynotes for transposed modal scales (Ex.80).

Ex. 80 Transposition table for modal scales

Key Signature:	♮	♯	♯♯	♯♯♯	♯♯♯♯	♭	♭♭	♭♭♭
Ionian	C	G	D	A	E	F	B♭	E♭
Dorian	D	A	E	B	F♯	G	C	F
Phrygian	E	B	F♯	C♯	G♯	A	D	G
Lydian	F	C	G	D	A	B♭	E♭	A♭
Mixolydian	G	D	A	E	B	C	F	B♭
Aeolian	A	E	B	F♯	C♯	D	G	C

Reading the table: first look to the key signature of the music, and then determine its keynote, with the aid of the following explanation:

The Key Signature. If the melody is not based on a transposed mode (as those in Chapter One) there will be no key signature, nor recurring sharps or flats in the notation.   When it is transposed, its key signature will either be stated or can be deduced from the sharps or flats that consistently occur.

The Keynote. Generally this is the note on which the melody ends.   But a word of caution regarding the keynotes of traditional folk tunes, notably those hailing from distant sources.   In these, as opposed to the more popular folk songs, the keynotes are not always readily identifiable.   In order that their verses, particularly intermediate ones, will unfold in a continuous and circular manner, the keynote is often held at bay and sometimes avoided.   For example, the last note in the melody of 'Cock Robin' could have been F sharp or B for the first and successive verses, leaving the keynote E for the end of the last verse.   When, in written folk songs, the keynote is side-stepped in this way, its identity is not obvious and may be subject to individual interpretation.

Assuming that the key signature and keynote are known, look down the column under the given key signature to the keynote in question: to the left of this is the name of the mode.   If the melody has a key signature of one sharp and a keynote A, look for A in the column under this key signature, and to the left of this note is the mode name, Dorian, in this case A-Dorian.

Practical transpositions

Practical transposition of written melodies can be approached in two ways. To illustrate these, the following song will be transposed from its present key C major (Ex.81) down a 3rd to A major.

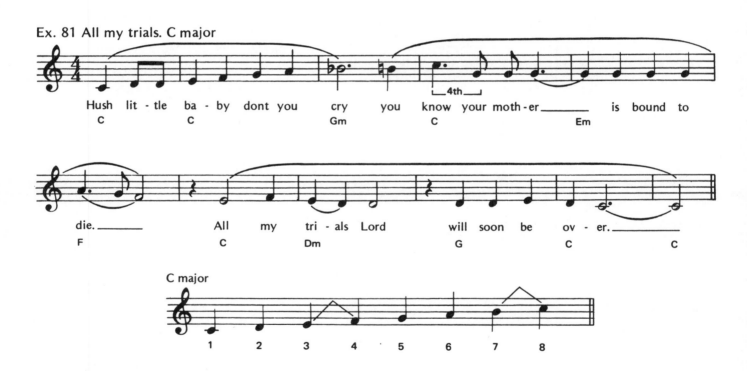

Ex. 81 All my trials. C major

Transposing this melody is comparatively easy because, apart from one leap of a 4th, it proceeds smoothly by step.   To conduct the transposition, the notes will first be regarded in terms of scale degrees, and then as a sequence of intervals.

Transposing by scale degrees, the opening phrase ascends from its tonic C, through the steps of C major to the flattened 7th degree, B flat.   Therefore the transposition in A major will begin on its tonic, now A, and ascend by step to the flattened 7th of that scale, G natural (Ex.82).

Ex. 82 All my trials. A major

A lit-tle tree grows in par-a-dise. Some peo-ple call it____ the tree of

| A | A | Em | A | C#m |

└─4th─┘

life._____ All my tri-als Lord will soon be ov-er._____

| D | A | Bm | E | A | A |

A major

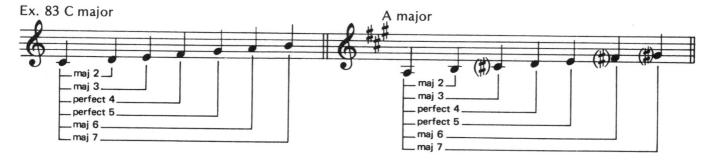

1   2   3   4   5   6   7   8

Review the C major melody and observe its leap of a 4th at the beginning of the second phrase. This is a leap from its tonic C to dominant G. Similarly, those notes in the transposition will also be tonic to dominant, A to E. Continuing the transposition along these lines, each note in the former melody is regarded as a scale degree in C major. Then by visual reference to both scales (or through mental calculation), the equivalent degree in A major is entered in the transposition.

Alternatively, and possibly working hand in hand with this method, is the second approach — considering the notes in terms of intervals. The first phrase of the C major version ascends in major and minor 2nds: C-D, D-E, E-F. When transposing this passage, the major/minor qualities of these intervals need not be taken into account as they will automatically match up with those in C major. To clarify this point, consider the qualities of the first three intervals: C-D and D-E are major 2nds; E-F is a minor 2nd. Likewise, the equivalent steps in A major, A-B, B-C sharp and C sharp-D are also two major 2nds and one minor 2nd (Ex.83).

Ex. 83 C major   A major

maj 2
maj 3
perfect 4
perfect 5
maj 6
maj 7

As well as assisting transposition, this major scale interval sequence provides a short cut to naming intervals. Consider the interval C-A. This is a 6th, but what kind, major or minor? Regard the bottom note as the tonic of the scale C major, and the upper note as its 6th degree. Bearing in mind the interval sequence for the major scale — 2nds, 3rds, 6ths and 7ths are major, 4ths, and 5ths are perfect — then the 6th C-A is immediately identifiable as a major interval. Consider another interval C-B flat. Again, regard the lower note as the tonic of C major and the upper for the moment as the 7th degree B. With the knowledge that this 7th interval, (C-B), is major 7th, then C-B flat, a semitone less, is a minor 7th.

Apply the same method and identify the quality of the 6th. A-F sharp. Regard A as the tonic of A major and F sharp as its 6th degree. The 6th interval in the major scale interval sequence is major, therefore A-F sharp is a major 6th. So it's a matter of learning the interval sequence for the major scale, then treating the lower note of the interval as the tonic of a major scale, and its upper note as a scale degree. If the upper note is an alteration such as C-B flat, then adjust the quality of the interval accordingly; C-B is a major 7th, therefore C-B flat is a minor 7th.

Progressions in other major keys

In keeping with the survey of chords in C major, those for the keys of G, D, A, E and F major are given in Ex.84 first as primary chord cadences and then as primary and secondary chord progressions. Reference to the relevant progression before the analysis of a classical instrumental work is undertaken will serve as a guide to its harmonic outlines. The chords may also be considered for folk song accompaniments and arrangements.

Ex. 84

G major

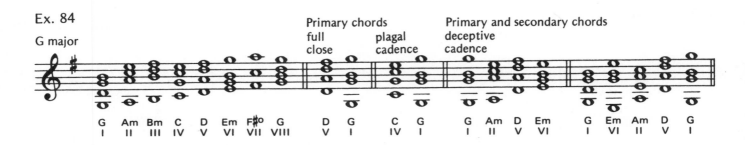

| G | Am | Bm | C | D | Em | F#o | G | D | G | C | G | G | Am | D | Em | G | Em | Am | D | G |
| I | II | III | IV | V | VI | VII | VIII | V | I | IV | I | I | II | V | VI | I | VI | II | V | I |

D major

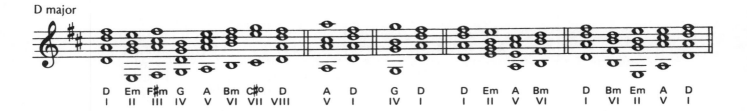

| D | Em | F#m | G | A | Bm | C#o | D | A | D | G | D | D | Em | A | Bm | D | Bm | Em | A | D |
| I | II | III | IV | V | VI | VII | VIII | V | I | IV | I | I | II | V | VI | I | VI | II | V | I |

A major

| A | Bm | C#m | D | E | F#m | G#o | A | E | A | D | A | A | Bm | E | F#m | A | F#m | Bm | E | A |
| I | II | III | IV | V | VI | VII | VIII | V | I | IV | I | I | II | V | VI | I | VI | II | V | I |

E major

| E | F#m | G#m | A | B | C#m | D#o | E | B | E | A | E | E | F#m | B | C#m | E | C#m | F#m | B | E |
| I | II | III | IV | V | VI | VII | VIII | V | I | IV | I | I | II | V | VI | I | VI | II | V | I |

F major

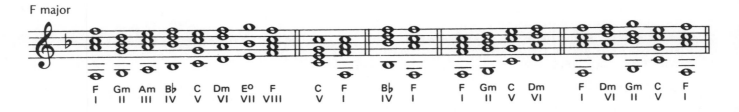

| F | Gm | Am | Bb | C | Dm | Eo | F | C | F | Bb | F | F | Gm | C | Dm | F | Dm | Gm | C | F |
| I | II | III | IV | V | VI | VII | VIII | V | I | IV | I | I | II | V | VI | I | VI | II | V | I |

Transposing chord progressions

Chord symbols are a positive boon. In one concentrated character they signify the chord's letter name, its quality and the altered or additional notes it contains. More to the point, chord symbols make for speedy transpositions of chord accompaniments. In fact, transposing chord progressions it terms of their symbols is so direct that, with practice, it can become spontaneous. In parallel with the melody for 'All my trials', the accompaniment for that song will now be transposed by exchanging the symbols for its chords in C major for those in A major.

Ex. 85 All my trials C major

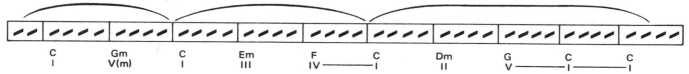

From its tonic chord Cmajor the progression takes in its sweep the two other primary chords in the key, Fmajor and Gmajor plus III and II secondary chords Eminor and Dminor. That 'borrowed' chord Gminor is adjusted to accommodate B flat in the melody, viz Gmajor — G, B, D; Gminor — G, B flat, D.

Transposing the progression to A major, the complete range of chord symbols for the key of C major are written out with their chord numbers. Beneath these are placed the corresponding chord symbols for A major. The transposition is then conducted by direct cross reference (Ex.86).

Chord numbers	I	II	III	IV	V	VI	VII	VIII
Initial key. C major	C	Dm	Em	F	G	Am	B°	C
Transposition. A major	A	Bm	C♯m	D	E	F♯m	G♯°	A

Ex. 86 All my trials A major

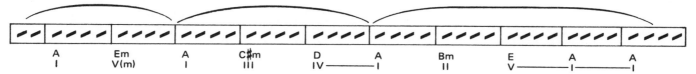

Just as the initial progression began with its tonic chord, Cmajor, the transposition begins with the corresponding chord, Amajor. The next chord in the C major progression is the altered dominant Gminor. Reference to the chord table shows the dominant chord in the key of A major is Emajor, in this case converted to Eminor. This procedure is continued for the remainder of the transposition: each chord in C major is exchanged for the corresponding chord in A major as shown in the table.

Now a phrase from an instrumental piece will be transposed from its original key, F major, down a 4th to C major. The scales for these keys are given in Ex.87a, but the aim is to refer to them as little as possible, transposing less in terms of scale degrees and more by interval correlation.

Ex. 87a

Ex. 87b
F major

Allegretto   M. Giuliani

A provisional glance over the music notation often reveals short cuts to its transposition. For example, the bass line in Ex.87b descends for the most part by step. Since the transposition for this line is straightforward, it can be done first, leaving the upper line until later. Beginning on F the tonic, the bass descends by step to B flat in bar 5, then ascends via the leading-note E to the tonic once more. The transposition of this line will have the same interval pattern, now C to C (Ex.88).

Ex. 88
C major

Allegretto   M. Giuliani

The bass line could of course be transposed bar by bar in conjunction with the melody. But in this excerpt it is far easier to do it in one swoop. Short cuts to the transposition of the upper line are also possible — namely through the exchange of triads. The F major melody begins with an arpeggio of its tonic chord, Fmajor — F, A, C, with two passing notes B natural and D. Then the transposition will begin with its tonic chord, Cmajor — C, E, G. The two passing notes, F sharp and A in the first bar of Ex.88, are inserted as major 2nds above their respective triad notes. In the second bar there is another opportunity to transpose in terms of triads with passing notes. The F major melody ascends from its bass note E, through the arpeggio Eminor — E, G, B. Similarly the transposition is an arpeggio built on its bass note B, or Bminor — B, D, F sharp. The remainder of the transposition is conducted when possible by the exchange of arpeggiated chords in F major with those in C major; or by transposing individual notes from the F major melody down a perfect 4th to those in C major.

When, as in the first two bars of this study, a triad is formed from a group of notes, that chord may be transposed in its entirety thus saving laborious cross reference to the scales. Passing notes can then be transposed in relation to the triad notes. For example, B natural and G sharp in Ex.87b are alien to the key of F major; but as they are attached to F major scale notes, they can be transposed laterally in terms of major/minor 2nds.

The intention behind this transposition was to show how initial observations will lighten the process. A longer way round is to proceed by step with constant cross reference to the scales. But think how uphill and tedious this would be over a lengthy composition. The first approach, that is transposing by chords and intervals, not only involves less effort, it also promotes a deeper understanding of the music's components and structure.

5: INVERSIONS

Through most of the foregoing chord progressions, the roots of the triads were linked as bass lines over which the other chord notes arose in vertical formations or branched out into horizontal melodies. With their roots lowermost, the chords or voice parts had a succession of underlying pivots to guide them and reinforce their cadences. Stable structures, yes, but with bass lines that contribute little in the way of melodic interest. Should the function of the bass be merely to serve as a stabilising force for short melodic spans, then root notes only will suffice. But over longer durations, a bass line of just root notes is liable to slump into laborious, angular strides.

Few instrumental pieces or song accompaniments rely solely on the roots of the chords for their bass lines. Like the melodies they support, bass lines are formed from notes within and outside the harmony. The middle and upper notes of the triads are assigned to them, and between these are placed passing notes unrelated to the chords. Then as melodies in their own right, the bass lines run alongside as complementary voices, taking over when the upper lines pause, and may sometimes hold the principal melodic interest throughout.

When the root of the triad is lowermost, that triad is in *root position*. Sturdy and evenly structured with ascending 3rds, root position chords generally set the harmony initially on its way. After the first step or so the root may then be transferred, leaving the middle note of the chord to be the bass as a *1st inversion* (Ex.89a).

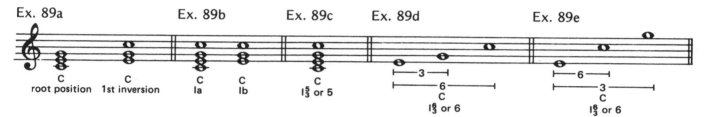

With its root C removed and placed an octave higher, the middle note E of Cmajor is now the bass as a 1st inversion (Ex.89a). Nevertheless, C retains its status as the root of the chord: the lower note E is simply an alternative bass note.

To distinguish between root position chords and 1st inversions in notation, a root position chord is sometimes denoted by a lower case 'a', and a 1st inversion with 'b' (Ex.89b). Alternatively, the chords may be denoted in terms of their interval layouts. With intervals of a 3rd and 5th, a root position chord is indicated by $\frac{5}{3}$ or simply 5 (Ex.89c); similarly, a 1st inversion with intervals of a 3rd and 6th is indicated by $\frac{6}{3}$ or 6 (Ex.89d). These symbols do not always specify the exact placing of the upper chord notes relative to the bass. Ex.89e has the upper note of its compound 3rd (E-G) above the 6th (E-C). Despite this apparent reversal, the symbol $\frac{6}{3}$ still applies.

Although the harmony may be figured in detail, the symbols for root position chords are often omitted. It is then taken for granted that the chords without accompanying symbols are in root position.

1st inversion triads in C major

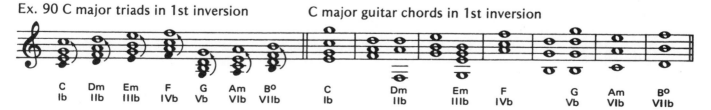

Ex. 90 C major triads in 1st inversion   C major guitar chords in 1st inversion

Ex. 91 Study in C

F. Sor

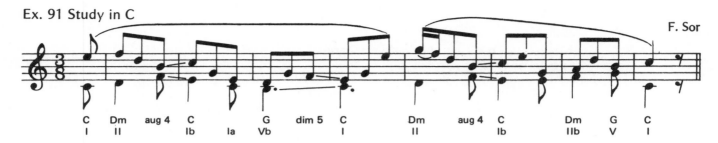

C	Dm	aug 4	C		G	dim 5	C		Dm	aug 4	C		Dm	G	C
I	II		Ib	Ia	Vb		I		II		Ib		IIb	V	I

Play the bass line of Ex.91 separately and notice how the roots and middle notes of Cmajor, Dminor and Gmajor are alternated as a counter melody for the upper line. Even though both parts have melodic individuality, they complement each other and maintain overall harmonic stability. This is ensured by the firm tonal anchorage, the keynote C fixed in the bass at the beginning of the phrase and at its full close ending; and the decisive resolution of the three tritones by contrary motion.

Though not so obvious in this example, but still a necessary consideration, is the difference in sound of a root position chord and a 1st inversion. The equilibrium of a triad is undermined when its root is transferred because it is no longer a composite of uniform parts, namely 3rds. Certainly the 3rd and 6th in a 1st inversion blend, but its stark sounding 4th ruffles the chord. Compare the sound of the two formations in Ex.89a and notice that the 1st inversion has not the composure of the evenly distributed notes in the root position chord.

And yet the less settled sounds of 1st inversions are an asset. These, plus the next inversion, offer a contrast to the staunchness of root position chords, tempering their clarity of sound by way of harmonic shading.

The 2nd inversion

If the root and middle note of a triad are inverted, its former upper note or 5th will be the bass as a *2nd inversion* (Ex.92).

Ex. 92

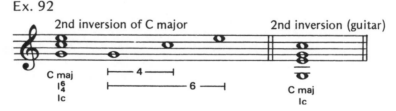

2nd inversion of C major   2nd inversion (guitar)

C maj
$\begin{smallmatrix}6\\4\end{smallmatrix}$
Ic

C maj
Ic

With intervals of a 4th and 6th, the 2nd inversion is denoted by a lower case 'c' or $\begin{smallmatrix}6\\4\end{smallmatrix}$. Although Ex.92 suggests a derivation of Cmajor in root position, a 2nd inversion should not be regarded strictly in this way. The *sound* of a 2nd inversion is unlike a chord with the same notes in root position. A chord in root position is stable, but the topsy-turvy arrangement of a 2nd inversion is, though not exactly dissonant, unsettled, and noticeably so in a surrounding of mostly root position chords.

When comparing the sound of a 2nd inversion of Cmajor against the same chord in root position, they should not be played together as the tonic C, common to both, will predominate and obscure their difference in quality. Better that they are heard in a context which clearly distinguishes them. This is a *cadential six four-five three*, and in it a 2nd inversion decorates a full close or deceptive cadence (Exs.93).

Ex. 93a   Cadential $\begin{smallmatrix}6\\4\end{smallmatrix}$ $\begin{smallmatrix}5\\3\end{smallmatrix}$ Ex. 93b

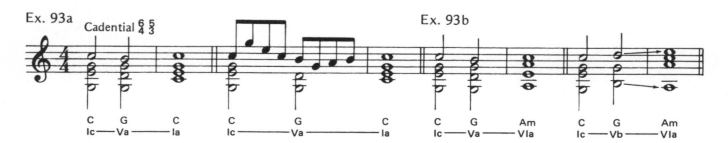

C	G	C		C	G	C		C	G	Am		C	G	Am
Ic	Va	Ia		Ic	Va	Ia		Ic	Va	VIa		Ic	Vb	VIa

Shown first as a block chord progression, then melodically embellished, Ex.93a has a 2nd inversion (the tonic chord) preceding a full close. In Ex.93b the same chord is followed by two deceptive cadences, the latter being more assertive in that its parts move by contrary motion.

Resolution and rest is most felt when it is preceded by irresolution. The sombre $\frac{6}{4}$ chord generates tension, the $\frac{5}{3}$ chord provides release. Combined, these contrasting effects enhance the sway of a full close or deceptive cadence. In addition, the $\frac{6}{4}$ with its dominant bass note acts as a substitute for the dominant chord, thereby lending harmonic variety to the cadence.

Ex. 94 Minuet

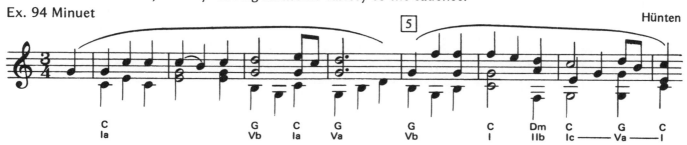

The first of the two phrases in Ex.94 pauses on a half close, the second ends with a cadential $\frac{6}{4}$ $\frac{5}{3}$. Between these cadences, 1st inversions and root position chords are freely mixed both for vertical harmonic variation and to shape a lyrical bass line. So individual is this lower part that at one point it conflicts with the melody. In the fifth bar, the repeated melody note F coincides with two bass notes in disgruntled intervals of a compound minor 7th (G-F), and a diminished 5th (B-F). Impervious to this dissension, the upper note F stubbornly keeps its hold into the sixth bar where it is then urged by Cmajor to succumb in downward resolution. While the melody continues its descent, the bass line rises to the dominant G of the 2nd inversion. On an accented beat and at the close of the phrase, the 2nd inversion withholds the arrival of the dominant, and in doing so heightens expectancy before the forthcoming full close.

Ex. 95

Through his economic deployment of root position and 1st inversion chords Giuliani cunningly alternates the melodic interest between the bass and treble lines, or distributes it equally across both parts. For the first three bars the bass holds the centre of attention, then with the resolution of the diminished 5th, the upper line comes into play. This Cmajor arpeggio and the two 6th intervals following are echoed by a similar pattern, the Gmajor arpeggio in bar 6 with two corresponding 6ths and an octave D. From the octave C in bar 9 each part goes its own way: the bass descends via a passing note B flat and the melody rises to the accented note G in bar 10. In conflict with its bass (a compound minor 7th A-G), the melody submits and falls a step to complete a consonance, the interval A-F in the 1st inversion of Fmajor. Next to this is a second inversion of Cmajor, but not from a cadential $\frac{6}{4}$ as there is no dominant chord to support it. A *passing* $\frac{6}{4}$, it maintains the continuity of the parts without drawing them into a cadence.

Resembling a 2nd inversion of Cmajor, the first chord in bar 12 is in fact a decorated dominant. Its accented upper note C is a retention from the foregoing chord F sharp diminished, bridging Dminor to Gmajor. Where the cadential $\frac{6}{4}$ does arise, and noticeably too, is in the final bar for the concluding cadence.

1st and 2nd inversions in other major keys

Ex. 96

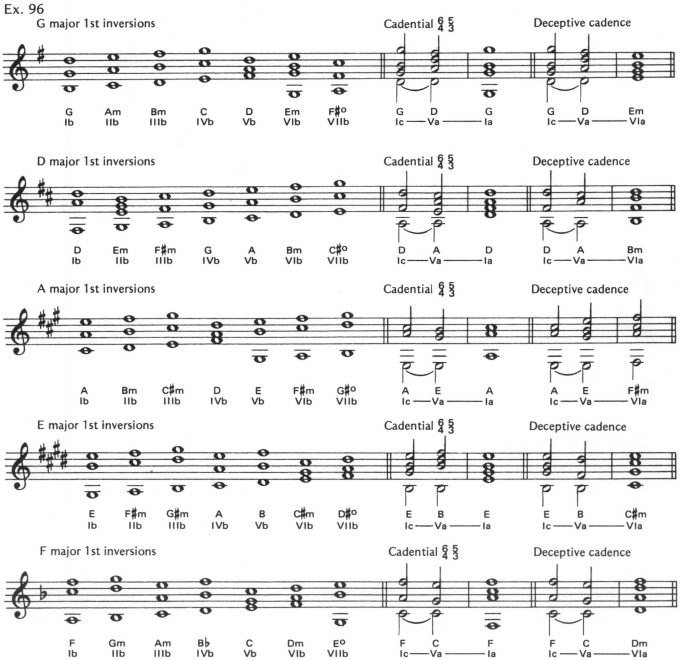

Inversions in G major

Ex. 97 Minuet

J. S. Bach

Partnered by its nimble waltz-like melody, the bass departs from the tonic G, ascends by step to the third bar then backtracks to the tonic. Not only do the inversions in bars 2 and 4 permit the bass a gradated rise and fall, they also widen its scope for movement. Though the melody from the beginning of bar 9 is a repeat of that in the opening bars, the bass line now descends in contrast to its earlier ascent. A subtle alteration, but one that provides the melody with different ground over which to retrace its route.

Inversions in D major

Ex. 98 Waltz

Anton Diabelli

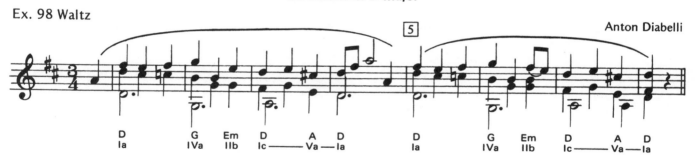

Guided by I-IV-V primary chords in the key of D major plus one secondary chord Eminor, the melody and bass line in Ex.98 start by flanking the inner line which descends by step to B, the lower note of the minor 6th in Gmajor. While the two upper lines continue as consecutive 6ths, the bass rises a tone to A in the 2nd inversion of Dmajor. The second phrase takes the same course as the first except for the melody note F near the end of bar 6. Conflicting with its bass G, this dissonance is immediately resolved by the downward step of the upper line to complete a 1st inversion of Eminor. To end the phrase is another $\begin{smallmatrix}6\\4\end{smallmatrix}$ $\begin{smallmatrix}5\\3\end{smallmatrix}$ but this time the parts terminate together on the tonic chord.

Summing up, major and minor chords in root position are the most stable chord formations. They provide a solid footing for the harmony's departure, they steer it decisively on course and secure it to the keynote in concluding cadences. Placed between root position chords, 1st inversions give a lyrical slant to the bass line, and vary the composure of the harmony. The somewhat morose sounding 2nd inversion appears either as a passing $\begin{smallmatrix}6\\4\end{smallmatrix}$ set between two firmer chords, or as an embellishment for a full close or deceptive cadence.

Before the letter names and major/minor qualities of inversions can be identified, their notes will need to be mentally reshuffled to see which one, placed in the bass, will give rise to successive 3rds. For instance, an arpeggio of ascending notes D, B, G would emerge with a little thought as the 2nd inversion of the triad Gmajor.

A final point: when possible, jot under the chords their names, C or C maj, A or Am, and under these enter their numbers and inversion symbols: Ia, VIa. Giving an added visual perspective on the harmony, they will aid your appraisal of its makeup and sounds.

6: MINOR KEYS

During the 17th century, the major and its sister scale, the *minor*, supplanted the modes as the principal bases for Western composition. From the major and minor tone-semitone series, a system emerged for classifying intervals, chords and chord progressions around a central note. Known as the 'diatonic' system, it has served as a pool of harmonic resources for composers up to, and in some cases beyond, the closing years of the 19th century.

One of the greatest assests of the diatonic system is its uniformity. Much said of the major applies to the minor. The minor's scale degrees have the same names as those given to the major; minor key chords are likewise built with 3rds, and they too are paired as perfect and half close cadences. Where the two scales differ is in their foundations, their layout of tones and semitones. In some compositions these differences are hardly noticeable; in others they are as marked as black and white. Before comparing chords built from these scales and music based on them, there are the steps of the minor to cover. These come in two principal forms, the *melodic* and *harmonic* minor. The most important is the harmonic minor scale, the basis for minor key chord construction (Ex.99).

Ex. 99 Scale of A harmonic minor

A hybrid, the harmonic minor is composed of elements from the Aeolian mode and major scale. From its tonic to 6th degree, the tone-semitone order of the harmonic minor is identical to the same portion of the Aeolian mode. Therefore the minor, like the Aeolian, ascends with restraint across the semitone step at its 2nd to 3rd degrees B-C, Ex.99. The 7th degree is sharpened so that the harmonic minor, like the major, will step purposely across the semitone from the leading-note to upper tonic.

Ex. 100

In addition to its minor 3rd, another factor distinguishes the harmonic minor from the major: its semitone step at the 5th to 6th degrees. When the two scales are compared on the same tonic (as in Ex.100), the minor with its semitone step, E-F sounds less determined at that stage of its ascent than the major with its more forthright whole-tone step, E-F sharp.

This is not to say that minor key compositions are by nature essentially sad. Charged with spirited rhythms, rapid arpeggios and fleeting scale passages, they can be just as sprightly as their major key counterparts. It is in the slow or leisurely paced pieces that the minor's plaintive and sometimes romantic side is so often revealed. Then the Aeolian strain makes its presence felt, subduing the harmony with minor 3rds, and restraining the ascent of melodic passages as they cross these intervals (Ex.101).

Ex. 101 Ecossaise   M. Giuliani

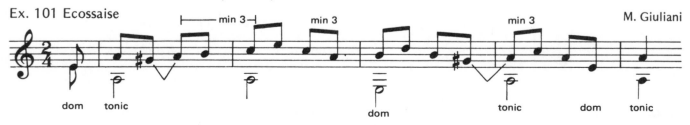

Since the leading-note and tonic in the first bar of Ex.101 are common to A major and A harmonic minor, we cannot say as yet which of the two scales the melody is based on. Over the following ascending steps, though, there is no such ambiguity; that telling minor 3rd is clearly from a minor scale. Had it been a major melody its upward leap at that point would be far more determined (Ex.102).

Ex. 102 Ecossaise (A major)

With major 3rds (A-C sharp), this modified major version is considerably more assertive. Yet despite the former's minor 3rds, that is not really a mournful tune for it has assertive forces to compensate. One is the mutual attraction of the dominant and tonic, E-A, and the other is the leading-note urging the melody forward to its tonic.

Accidental notes

The degrees of the major and minor scales are called *diatonic* notes, meaning that they are components of diatonic scales. Both versions of 'Ecossaise' are composed only of diatonic notes, the first from the scale of A minor, the second from A major. However, there are many major and minor compositions which include notes from outside the range of their particular scales. These outsiders or *chromatic* notes are drawn into a diatonic framework for colouring or to broaden the music's scope. Then in which category, diatonic or chromatic, should the 7th degree of the minor scale be placed? It appears to fall between two stools: it is an important scale note and yet it has a separate sharp sign which apparently brands it an outsider or a chromatic note. If the scale of A harmonic minor had a key signature of one sharp, its 7th degree would be unquestionably diatonic. The reason why the sharp is not stated as a key signature is because this note is not always sharpened in the composition. Nonetheless, the raised 7th degree is treated as a diatonic note, but with a special status. With a sharp sign exclusive to itself, it is called an *accidental* note.

There are three other points relating to accidentals: first, the sharp sign not only applies to its accompanying note but to a repeat of that note within the same bar (Ex.103a).

Ex. 103a   Ex. 103b   Ex. 103c

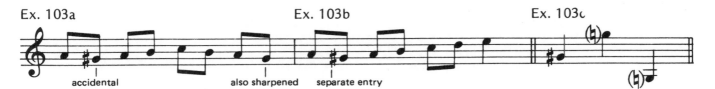

Second, if the 7th degree is to be sharpened in the next bar, another sharp sign will need to be entered there (Ex.103b). Third, the sharp sign only applies to notes of the same pitch within the bar. In Ex.103c, the sharp sign against the first note does not apply to the other two G notes of different pitches. Should it be necessary to sharpen these, they would need separate sharp signs.

Where the 7th degree is not generally sharpened is at positions detached from, and not bearing upon, the tonic. In a stepwise descending passage, for example, a natural 7th degree will permit the line to gravitate gracefully by not imposing a sharp to counteract its downward tread. Then part of another minor scale is brought into play, the *melodic* minor (Ex.104).

Ex. 104 A melodic minor

A basis for minor key melodies, notably vocal lines, the melodic minor has two accidentals in its ascending half, the raised 6th and 7th degrees (F sharp and G sharp, Ex.104). By raising the 6th as well as the 7th degrees, the whole-tone step across those notes is more vocally accessible than the corresponding step of 1½ tones in the harmonic minor (F-G sharp). In the steps of the Aeolian mode the descending half of the melodic minor falls sedately under its own weight through the natural 7th and 6th degrees.

Ex. 105 Minuet

Purcell

Even with four separate sharp signs in the notation of Ex.105, little effort would be saved by lumping these together as a G sharp signature. That would necessitate entering natural signs against the two G notes in the bass (bars 2 and 6). As it is, the sharp signs are entered as necessary, leaving the G bass notes to be played as naturals. The descending bass line A to E, across the first phrase is one of the few and far between examples of melodic minor instrumental music. In guitar music particularly, the harmonic minor far outweighs the melodic form which is rarely used, and then, only in part. The G note in bar 6 is natural so as not to highlight the tonic prematurely. Reserved for where it will carry most impact, the sharpened 7th degree precedes the final tonic note in the full close cadence, more of which will be shown in *minor key harmony*.

Minor key harmony

Corresponding with the three primary chords in major keys, minor key primary chords are built on the 1st, 4th and 5th degrees of the minor scale (Ex.106).

Ex. 106

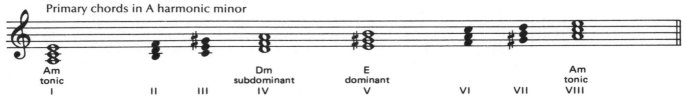

Chords I and IV in the minor key have lower intervals of minor 3rds, and outer intervals of perfect 5ths. Therefore these are minor triads. The dominant contains the leading-note, and with a lower interval of a major 3rd, E-G sharp, this is a major chord.

Extending the earlier comparison of A major and A minor scales to their primary chords, I-IV-V for A major and A minor are placed side by side in Ex.107.

Ex. 107

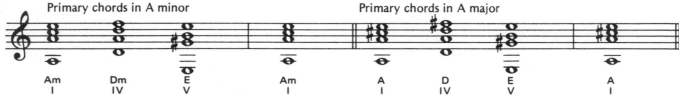

In the light of major key primary chords, those in the minor are noticeably subdued. Yet between the more sombre shades of the minor key's tonic and subdominant, the dominant chord shines through, its leading-note urging the harmony forward in a full close cadence (Ex.108).

Ex. 108

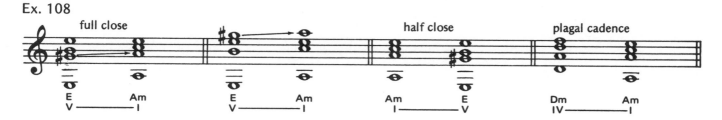

Ex. 109

Allegro

M. Giuliani

Mellow the tonic and subdominant chords may be, but by no means do they dampen the spirit of Ex.109. Fragmented into lively arpeggios, it romps ahead with all the alacrity of an up-tempo study in a major key. The rhythmic pattern set by the opening arpeggio Aminor is repeated in the second bar across the subdominant chord, and again in bar 3 on the dominant. Near the end of the third bar the bass line begins to descend and continues with downward steps into the next bar through C, the bass of the 1st inversion of Aminor. Preparing for the return of the opening two bars, the bass line steps down to B in the 2nd inversion of Emajor — E, G sharp, B with an added note D.

Another arpeggio merits attention, the dominant in the first half of bar 8. This contains an alien note A (marked by the asterisk) lingering from the 2nd inversion in the bar before. As we shall see in the next chapter, this note is deliberately repeated out of place so as to tickle the harmony near the end of a phrase with a dissonance (A-B). At the last moment the rightful note, G sharp, ousts the intruder, thus restoring stability to the dominant chord for the concluding full close.

Minor key secondary chords

Like major key secondary chords, those in the minor key are built on the 2nd, 3rd, 6th and 7th degrees of the minor scale (Ex.110a).

Ex. 110a

Ex. 110b

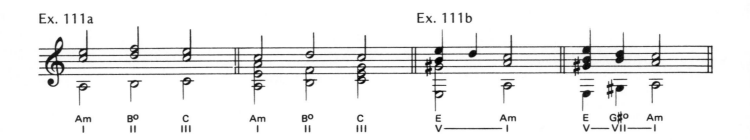

With two minor 3rds and an outer interval of a diminished 5th, II the supertonic is a diminished triad, Bdiminished. Although III, the mediant contains the scale's 7th degree, this chord rarely precedes the tonic, therefore the 7th degree is unlikely to be raised. If it is, the mediant will have two major 3rds forming an outer interval of an augmented 5th, hence its classification, *augmented* — C augmented or indicated with a plus sign C+. Because of its dissonant augmented 5th interval, the augmented triad is a discord. To resolve it, one note of the augmented 5th is usually positioned in the upper line which then rises or falls to complete a concord (Ex.110b).

So the harmonic range of the minor embodies four different types of triad: major, minor, diminished and augmented. Rarely are all types used within the scope of a single composition, but they are there in reserve, ready to vary the harmony or the supporting lines of a repeated melody. Placed between or substituting primary chords, II will bridge I to III (Ex.111a), and VII can be linked with or substitute V (111b).

Ex. 111a   Ex. 111b

Ex. 112 Gavotte (A minor)

J. S. Bach

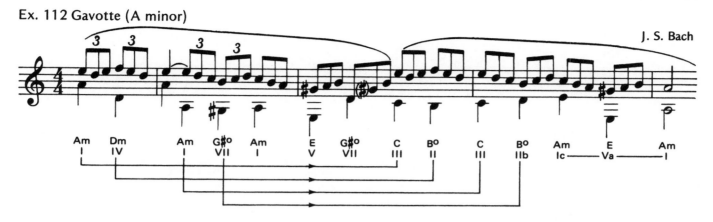

From the second Gavotte in Bach's lute suite in A minor, Ex.112 has two phrases of virtually the same melody but with different bass lines. From the melody alone chords are implied, and from these chords bass notes are taken to underpin each triplet group. The first triplet has two outer notes E and an inner passing note D. To establish the keynote of the piece, this triplet is harmonised with A, the root of the tonic chord. Now these two outer notes are also part of the triad Cmajor, the root note of which is used for the same triplet at the beginning of the second phrase. Turning to the second triplet in the opening phrase, its harmony notes are again the outer ones, now F and D. Which bass note will support these, the root of Dminor or Bdiminished? Bach has chosen the primary chord for this triplet leaving the secondary chord for its repeat.

Back to the first phrase and its third triplet, Aminor. This has two notes in common with its substitute Cmajor. The root of Aminor harmonises the triplet in the first phrase (reaffirming the tonic); and the root of Cmajor harmonises the same notes in the second phrase (for variation). Similarly, the fourth chord G sharp diminished has two notes in common with the implied Bdiminished chord in the second phrase. G sharp diminished is more suited to the first triplet on the strength of its bass leading-note rising to the tonic; while the lower note of Bdiminished fits equally well into the ascending bass line at that position. The golden rule, then: vary the harmony of a repeated melody.

Inversions in A minor

Ex. 113

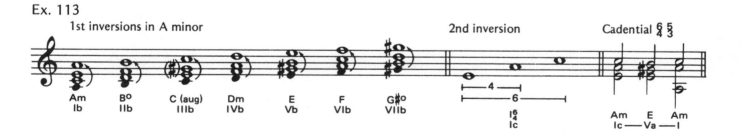

Ex. 114

Andantino

F. Carulli

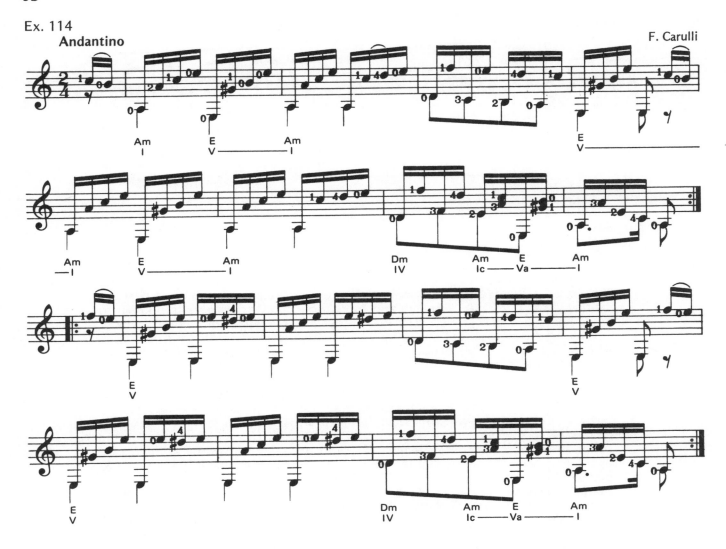

Returning to the primary chords in A minor but now with inversions, Ex.114 has four phrases centred mainly on tonic and dominant arpeggios. After an introductory V-I establishing the key, the first phrase splits into two lines descending in compound 3rds to rest on the dominant chord at a half close. The second phrase begins by repeating the opening bars of the first, and is then drawn through the subdominant to end with a cadential $\begin{smallmatrix}6&5\\4&3\end{smallmatrix}$. Notice how neatly this 2nd inversion falls into place: it snugly accommodates C from the descending melody (which incidentally reflects the melody's descent in the corresponding bar above); and with its dominant bass note, it anticipates the dominant chord for the ensuring full close.

After a dominant pedal bass E and repeated dissonance D sharp-E in the melody, the third phrase descends in compound 3rds to a half close; and the final phrase, with the same dominant pedal, ends with a cadential $\begin{smallmatrix}6&5\\4&3\end{smallmatrix}$.

For all its simplicity, 'Andantino' is attractive and clearly symmetrical. Its symmetry lies in its balanced phrases and the cadences defining them. Reviewing these, the first phrase pauses with a comma at a half close. The second phrase ends decisively with a full stop, the full close. In the same manner, the third phrase falls to a half close, and the fourth ends with a full close. Four equidistant spans, the second balancing the first, and the fourth balancing the third in pendulum-like swings between the tonic and dominant chords.

Ex. 115 Aria from Partita in A minor

J. A. Logy

①

Am
I

F
VI

E
V

Am
Ib

Dm
IVb —————

E
V

②

mf

E
V

Am
Ib

F
VI or Dm
      IVb
V —————

G
♮VII ————— I

C

F
IV —————

G
V —————

C
I

E
V

Am
Ib

Dm
IV

E
V —————

Am
I

And now an intricate arrangement of inversions in an imaginative contrapuntal setting (Ex.115). Not only do the inversions contribute to the smooth rise and fall of the bass line, their harmonic shades merge vertically with the more distinct profiles of root position chords. When, however, the notes of inverted chords are given a horizontal emphasis, they sometimes elude specific definition. For example, the opening triad is clearly Aminor, but what of the chord immediately after this? It could be defined as Fmajor with its 3rd omitted and an upper E added; but it is more a liaison of three notes from three voice parts: C and E repeated from Aminor coinciding with F passing in the bass.

Another debatable chord is the one at the beginning of bar 6. Is this a 1st inversion of Dminor — D, F, A, with a passing note C; or Fmajor — F, A, C, with a passing note D? In context it appears as Fmajor or IV in IV-V-I, a bridge progression to the temporary new key chord Cmajor. Another indication marking the transition from the original key A minor to C major is the melody note G natural near the middle of bar 7. Had the music not shifted its tonal centre then that note, a step away from A, would have been sharpened. Returning to the original key A minor, the last phrase pauses half way through on the dominant chord then completes its journey via IV-V-I with C in the tonic chord omitted.

Transposition of the minor scales

Two other minor scales, E and D minor, are also popular for guitar instrumental music. In these, as in A minor, there are fewer demands on left hand fingering because each scale has two important notes produced by open strings. In E minor the important open-string notes are the 6th and 5th strings, notes E and A (the tonic and subdominant); and in D minor they are the 4th and 5th open-strings, notes D and A (tonic and dominant), Ex.116.

Ex. 116

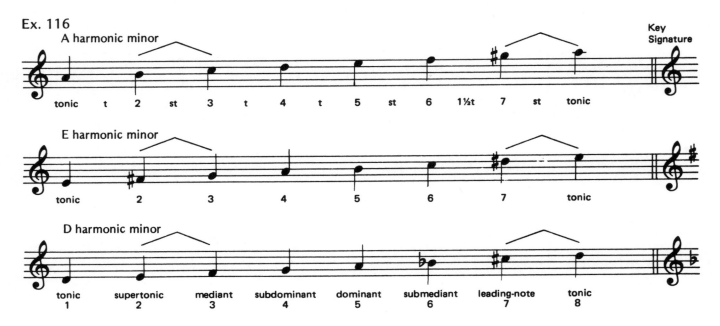

To concur with the tone-semitone order for the harmonic minor, E minor has its 2nd degree sharpened (so that there will be a semitone at its 2nd to 3rd degrees); and D minor has its 6th degree flattened (so that there will be a semitone at its 5th to 6th degrees). These adjustments are indicated in the key signatures shown on the right of the scales. The sharp signs indicating the raised 7th degrees are as usual, entered against the relevant notes.

Transposition of minor key harmony

Ex. 117

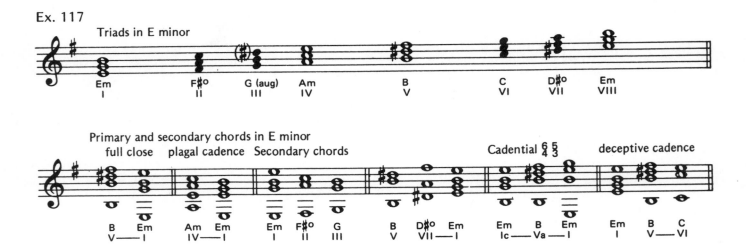

Ex. 118 Aria detta 'La Frescobalda'

G. Frescobaldi

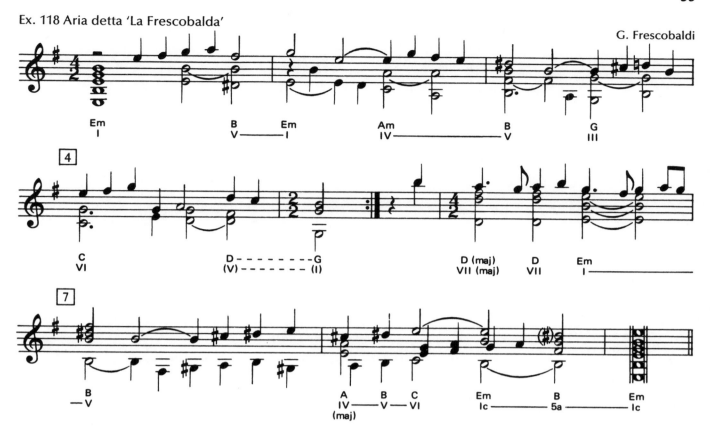

As distinct from 18th and 19th century vocal operatic arias, this 17th century instrumental aria is the theme for a set of variations. Since the work is mainly contrapuntal and involves a number of secondary chords, bearings will first be taken from its principal chord progressions. These are an introductory V-I at the beginning of the theme, its full close in the last bar, and two half close cadences IV-V bar 3, and I-V bar 7.

Supporting a graceful melody, the first chord suggests the key of E minor and this is confirmed by the bass leading-note rising to the tonic in bar 2. From here the hitherto vertical chords divide into three lines — two upper voices pausing at a half close, and the bass falling to the root of Gmajor in bar 3. The descent of this bass line from B to G is an imitation of its descent in the bar before from E to C. An important detail, for it shows that the melodic and rhythmic patterns are designed to balance and mean something to each other, and are not simply sketched in to maintain continuity. Bass and melody then pass through the chords Cmajor to Dmajor in bar 4. The latter chord assumes the role of a new dominant transferring the harmony from its original key chord Eminor to rest on another, Gmajor. Ending the phrase on Gmajor leaves the tonic chord in reserve for the beginning of the repeat.

Though the final phrase starts on Dmajor (bar 6), it returns smartly to its original tonic chord, followed by a half close. Near the end of the theme, and steered by a IV-V bass progression, the upper voices anticipate a full close. It doesn't happen, for at this position the tonic chord would curtail the phrase. Instead a deceptive cadence carries the lines through to a more natural and timely conclusion, a cadential $\begin{smallmatrix} 6 \\ 4 \end{smallmatrix} \begin{smallmatrix} 5 \\ 3 \end{smallmatrix}$

Ex. 119

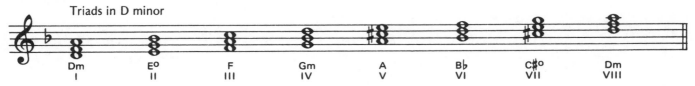

Triads in D minor

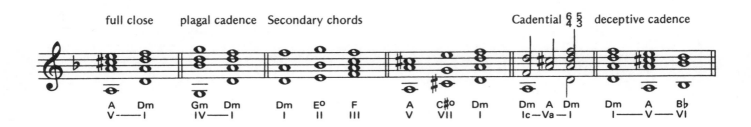

full close   plagal cadence   Secondary chords   Cadential $^6_4$ $^5_3$ deceptive cadence

Ex. 120 Minuet

Robert de Visée

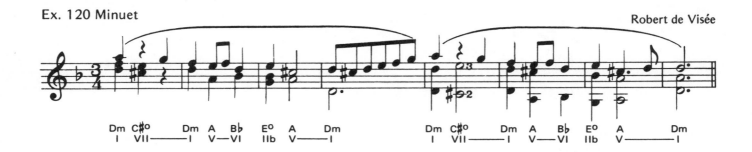

A movement from de Visée's Suite in D minor, Ex.120 has two four-bar phrases, the second a repeat of the first except that its bass line is lowered an octave. From the opening chord Dminor, the melody and its two subordinate lines pivot on C sharp diminished then back-step, converging as the two notes in the incomplete chord Dminor. The following deceptive cadence (V-VI) carries little impact due to the lack of density in its lower voice, and the omission of C sharp in the dominant chord. In the second phrase the tonic triad is now pronounced by C sharp in C sharp dim., and through the weight of a low bass line. As a finishing touch for the last full close, a decoration is added called an *anticipation*. This is the penultimate melody note D, a non-harmonic tone tailing C sharp in the dominant chord. As though impatient, this tonic note oversteps its harmony in anticipation of the ensuing tonic chord.

Identifying the minor scales

Key signatures are a mixed blessing. On the credit side, they state in one, those notes that are to be consistently sharpened or flattened. But they can be confusing in that they are not individually allocated to specific scales but are common to different types. To add to the problem there is a tendency to associate familiar key signatures with familiar scales — usually the ubiquitous majors. Presuming that a composition is major when its basis is quite something different will of course throw an attempt at analysing it way off the mark.

Consider the key signature of one flat, B flat. This has been associated with the key F major, with modal scale transpositions, and in the last example with D minor. To which of these scales this key signature would apply for a given composition can be deduced by observing certain factors in the music: its keynote, its leading-note, or if not this then the whole tone step from the 7th to 8th degrees as in the Aeolian or Dorian modes.

A case in point review the last example, de Visée's 'Minuet'. Its keynote is clearly D, being the first and last note of the bass line, and the last note of the melody. So far, then, we know that this scale has a tonic D, and that its key signature indicates B flat. With this knowledge plus the fact that each 7th degree is sharpened in the notation, then D minor heads the list as the scale basis. Keeping this scale in mind, consider others with the same tonic. D major can be rejected as that would entail a key signature of two sharps. Neither is it D-Aeolian or the Dorian mode as these approach their tonics with whole-tone steps. This music has a leading-note C sharp (the 7th degrees of the Aeolian or Dorian modes are not leading-notes; a leading-note is a semitone from the tonic of a major or minor scale). So the tell-tale accidentals, the tonic D and a key signature of one flat point with certainty to the scale of D minor.

Major and minor relationships

Certain major and minor scales are directly related through their common key signatures. G major and E minor are directly related, being the only major and minor scales with a key signature of one sharp. G major is called the *relative major* to E minor; and E minor is the *relative minor* to G major. By the same token, C major and A minor are directly related in that they are the only major and minor scales with no key signature. C major is the relative major to A minor; and A minor is the relative minor to C major (Exs.121).

Ex. 121a C major   Ex. 121b A harmonic minor

To calculate the relative minor's tonic from a given major scale, count up a 6th from that major's tonic. In Ex.121a the relative minor's tonic A is five steps above C, the tonic of the given major. To calculate the relative major's tonic from a given minor scale, count up a 3rd from the minor's tonic (Ex.121b). Two steps above the tonic of A minor is the tonic C for the relative major.

The direct relationship between a particular major and minor scale is more than just a theoretical bond. Admittedly both scales have different tonics and tone-semitone orders, but they are nevertheless drawn from virtually the same fund of notes. All the notes of C major are naturals, and all but one in A harmonic minor are naturals too. So it's the simplest thing to transfer a composition from its home based major key to the relative minor, or, as in Bach's 'Gavotte' (Ex.112), from minor to relative major.

Harmonically the major/minor relationship has a practical function too. Cast your mind back to the chord progressions in the key of C major, where VI or Aminor substituted I or Cmajor. Extending the major/minor scale relationship to triads built on the first and sixth notes of the major scale, VI is called the *relative minor* chord to the tonic major; conversely, in a minor key, III or Cmajor is the *relative major* chord to the tonic minor chord, Aminor.

Minor chords in modal folk song accompaniments

Despite the abundance of minor key instrumental music, the minor scale plays very little part in folk song tunes. A few Negro spirituals and American folk songs are based on the scale, but rarely, if ever, does it arise in traditional English ballads. Cecil Sharp brought up this point in one of his essays on English folk song.

"Personally I have never recovered an English folk song in a minor scale, and few have been recorded by other collecters. Minor folk airs are, no doubt, Aeolian that have been modernised by the addition of a leading-note. The minor is a very modern scale in art music, and lends itself more readily to harmonic effects than melodic". *"English Folk Song: Some conclusions". E.P. Publishing Ltd.*

The harmonic effects that he refers to are not confined to minor key instrumental music. Chords derived from the harmonic minor scale are also used in the accompaniments for Aeolian and Dorian tunes. Chords I and V in both these modes are minor triads, and in the case of the Aeolian, IV is minor too (Ex.122).

Ex. 122

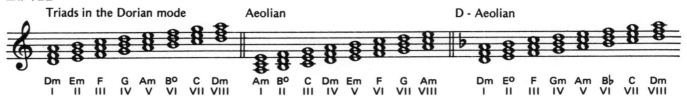

The essential difference between modal and minor harmony is that triads built on modal scales contain no leading-notes. Each mode in Ex.122 has as its dominant, a minor chord (and not a major quality as in a minor key); and VII is major (and not a diminished quality as in a minor key).

Ex. 123

In addition to V-I (and IV-I), a progression of VII-I is particularly suited to modal harmony, emphasising the Aeolian and Dorian's whole-tone steps to their upper tonics. Moreover, as VII has two notes in common with V, one may substitute the other, melody permitting (Ex.124, see also Exs.7 and 8).

Ex. 124 Sinner Man

To enhance a modal accompaniment, omit the middle notes from its chords. Deprived of these, the accompaniment will loose its major/minor identity and take on a plaintive air, the result of combinations of 4ths and octaves. This may be detected in the chords for 'Sinner Man' where the arpeggios loosely defined as Dminor have their middle notes F omitted, hence D, A, D.

A final point regarding the arrangements of the accompaniments: running arpeggios are in keeping with the capers of Sinner Man, but in slower moving lines this stock effect may force the pace, or pall over successive verses. Softly stroked chords without fanciful distractions will allow the words and melody to breath, and the story to unfold in its own time.

7: THE SUSPENSION AND THE DOMINANT 7th

Suspensions

Most of the melodies dealt with so far have progressed pretty much in harmony with their accompaniments. Neither lagging noticeably behind nor leaping ahead, they kept pace with either a supporting chord progression or other adjacent lines. Such balanced designs are ideal for short periods, but over extended durations their unvarying equanimity is liable to languish through lack of bite.

Dissonance of course is one invigorating ingredient; and if a note in the harmony is thrown out of phase, that will create rhythmic cross-currents through the lines. One such displaced note is called a *suspension*, and from it both dissonance and rhythmic excitement is produced. A note from either the principal melody or a subordinate part is held over or repeated while the concurrent lines or chords continue unimpeded. Out of place, the suspended note disrupts the pulse of the music and sparks a dissonance as it strikes against its alien harmony. To correct this imbalance, the harmony is then withheld while the delayed melody catches up so that all lines can continue reunited.

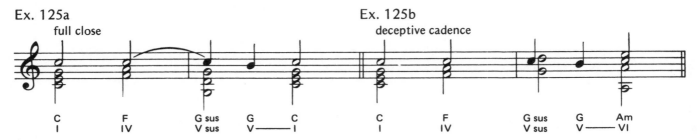

The crotchet C in the upper line at the beginning of the second bar in Ex.125a is suspended from Fmajor while an incomplete chord of Gmajor (G, D), is played underneath. Alien to its accompanying chord, the suspension conflicts with D below (a minor 7th, D-C) and G (a perfect 4th, G-C, which in a harmonic context has a dissonant effect too). To resolve the discord the voice with the suspension yields to its harmony, and in falling to B, completes the chord Gmajor thus restoring calm to the harmony and equilibrium to the rhythm.

This suspension is positioned near the end of the phrase as an ornament for a full close. That in Ex.125b occurs in the middle of the phrase to enhance its sway. Here the discord is more pronounced because the infiltrating suspension asserts itself as a reiterated note and not as one withheld. Moreover, poised in the centre of the harmony a major 2nd results (C-D), a sharper dissonance than the minor 7th in the former suspended chord.

As C is sounded in the preceding chord before it takes effect as a suspension, one half of the dissonance is, so to speak, played before the other. Without changing its position in the progression, this note, designated to be the suspension, prepares the dissonance and as such is called a *preparation*.

Minor key suspensions

Ex. 126 Suspension in A minor

Am	Dm	E sus	E	Am
I	IV	V	V	I

(See also Ex. 115, bars 11 - 12)

Decorating the full close in A minor is the suspension A, again a reiterated note and not one held across. Coinciding with the anticipated dominant chord Emajor, a major 2nd (A-B) and perfect 4th (E-A) results. Dutifully prepared as an essential (component) note of Dminor, the dissonance is then resolved by the downward step of the middle voice to complete the dominant chord.

Ex. 127 Diferencias sobre Guardame las vacas

Luys de Nárvaez

The first of six variations or *diferencias* on the Spanish folk song 'Guard the cows', Ex.127 shows the bass line on which the other variations are based. The chords emerging from this bass line are fragmented as arpeggios and set into melodic passages with additional passing notes from the scale of A minor. Near the end of the second line, the melody note A is suspended a compound 4th above its bass E. The effect of this stark perfect 4th is pronounced by the fact that the descending melody lingers on A instead of falling to the expected chord note G sharp. However, this deliberate delay enhances the phrase by imposing an incongruous 4th a moment before its conclusion on a harmonious 3rd.

Suspensions in other major and minor keys

Ex. 128

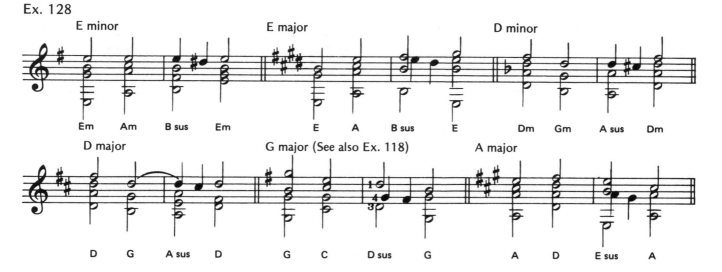

Suspensions in 17th century instrumental music usually coincide with the dominant chord. Viewing that chord vertically, the suspension can be regarded as its raised middle note, i.e. Gmajor-G, B, D; G suspended-G, C, D. But bear in mind that this is not an all embracing definition, for it states the position of the suspension only in relation to the notes in the dominant chord; whereas traditionally a suspension is a device bound into a broader horizontal framework — an ornament in a contrapuntal setting. Furthermore, a suspension is not always the middle note of a dominant chord, nor indeed is it confined to that chord. In the following excerpt there are a variety of suspensions and only one is resolved into the dominant chord, in this case the minor dominant in bar 8.

Ex. 129 Fantasia   Luys de Nārvaez

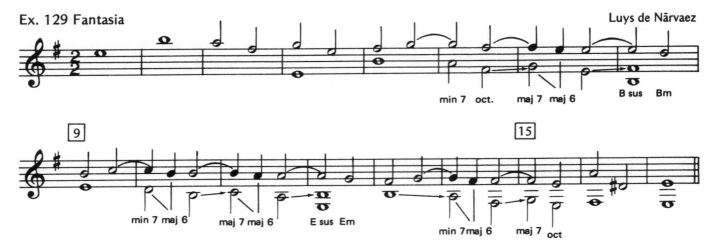

Extending the analysis of this fantasia from that given in Ex.29, its voice parts will now be regarded in terms of their suspensions. Not until the sixth bar does one arise, but from there they form a continuous chain. The first to appear is the upper note G held across the fifth bar line. Under this the counter line falls a tone to A, the lower note of a minor 7th. Unlike the previous resolutions where the lower lines remained stationary while the upper lines fell, here both move to a consonance, the octave F sharp in bar 6. Thereafter a succession of dissonances result from the ascending or descending steps in the counter melody, and are duly resolved by the ensuing descending steps of the upper line.

Ex. 130 Melancholy Galliard   J. Dowland

True to its name, an air of gloom pervades Ex.130 which the piquancy of three suspensions under the melody does little to alleviate. The first is the note D in the chord Amajor, suspended from the opening key chord Dminor. To resolve the major 2nd, D-E, the centre voice falls to C sharp, the middle note of the dominant chord. At a corresponding position in the next phrase is the second suspension, now held by Cmajor. Balancing these two phrases is a third, longer phrase with another suspension, prepared and resolved in the same manner as the first. The major chord in the last bar is a *tièrce de Picardie* — where a major tonic chord is used for a sectional ending or the conclusion of a minor key composition.

In short, a suspension has a twofold effect: a displaced note, it accentuates the *rhythm* and enlivens the harmony with its *dissonance.* Though the suspensions here were portrayed in traditional settings, they can also be used for present-day song accompaniments and instrumental arrangements to embellish the chords with a little ornamental inlay.

The dominant 7th

The most popular, and by now most jaded, discord in standard harmony is the *dominant 7th*. Keeping its hold through centuries of changing musical styles, the dominant 7th continues to thrive in popular music, traditional jazz, folk song accompaniments, rock and the blues.

Being a discord, the dominant 7th carries that much more impact than the three-note dominant concord from which it is derived. But in its strength lies its weakness; excessive and indiscriminate use of the chord has consequently blunted its edge. Yet thoughtfully employed, it will add extra impetus to a progression during its course, and reinforce cadences.

Ex. 131a Dominant 7th in C major   Ex. 131b

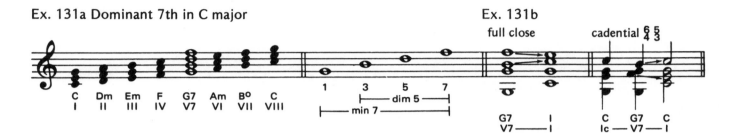

A full close with a dominant triad chord is resolute enough without the need of an extra note to boost it. Two forces combine, the compulsive step of the leading-note to tonic, and the bass leap from the dominant to tonic root. But when the dominant is capped with a 7th note, two dissonances result (Ex.131a). The resolution of these makes for a stronger progression than the dominant concord to tonic.

For the most effective resolution, the tritone B-F in the dominant 7th is resolved in contrary motion by the consonant interval in the tonic chord (Ex.131b). Then the tendencies for the upper part with the 7th note to fall and that with the leading-note to rise are both satisfied.

Like many discords, the dominant 7th came into being partly as a concord with an ingratiating 7th note, and partly through its tentative implementation as a self-contained discord. The works of Claudio Monteverdi (1576-1643) demonstrate the dominant 7th in both these lights. At the beginning of the second bar in Ex.132a, the 'Coronation of Poppeà, the dominant 7th is so carefully prepared and quitted that it is heard as the concord G major with an incidental passing note F. On the other hand, Monteverdi's works, renowned for their enterprising harmonies, often reveal unprepared discords too. Such is the dominant 7th in Ex.132b, a blatant vertical formation of G7 (minus its 5th note D) with an unprepared but correctly resolved 7th.

Ex. 132a from scene I   Ex. 132b   C. Monteverdi

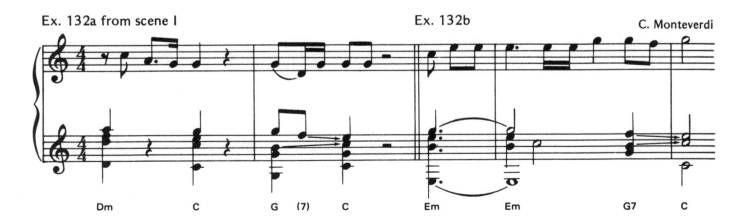

By the 18th century the dominant 7th had come into its own as a self-contained four-note discord. Either as a dominant chord with a passing 7th, or as a fully-fledged discord, it was, and still most commonly is; resolved by the tonic in a full close or the relative minor chord in a deceptive cadence (Ex.133).

Ex. 133 dominant 7ths in C major

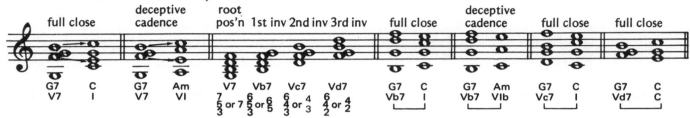

Ex.133 shows the dominant 7th in root position and then in each of its inversions. In root position it is denoted as V7, and its inversions are denoted either in terms of their interval layouts in respect to the bass or with letter symbols: V7b for a 1st inversion; V7c a 2nd inversion; V7d a 3rd inversion. In each progression the tritone is resolved by contrary motion.

Ex. 134 Study in C

Napolean Coste

Checked by three suspensions, the melody in the first phrase of Ex.134 is timed to converge with its ascending bass line on the dominant chord in bar 4. The first suspension, a repeated note F at the beginning of bar 2 (Csus.), is particularly interesting in that it is not attached to the dominant but to the tonic chord wherein it is resolved. This tonic chord, weakened by an octave 3rd, E-E, prepares the next suspension which is resolved by the downward step of the melody to complete a 1st inversion of Dminor. Following this is a *chromatic* chord, F sharp diminished, incorporated with the diatonic chords in the key to maintain the stepwise ascent of the bass line, and draw the phrase smoothly to a half close. Staying on the dominant chord, the second phrase is a repeat of the first except for its final cadence, a full close with a dominant 7th in root position.

Minor key dominant 7ths

Dominant 7ths in minor keys are just as forceful as those in major keys. In the key of A minor, the dominant 7th is the triad Emajor with an added 7th note, seven steps up from its root (Ex.135).

Ex. 135 dominant 7th A minor

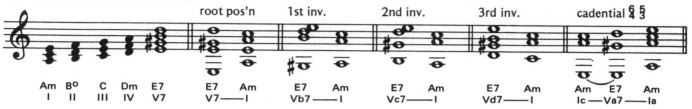

Dominant 7ths in other major and minor keys

Ex. 136

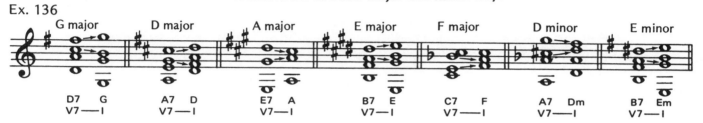

Familiar progressions in early 19th century guitar literature, the dominant 7ths with their resolutions in Ex.136 also abound in popular music, folk song accompaniments and rock progressions. One field of modern music where the dominant 7th not only enforces a full close but adds a distinctive tonal colour and effect is in the *Blues*.

The dominant 7th in the blues

Originally a black American folk art, the blues have since broadened and flourished first through jazz and recently in rhythm and blues, rock and roll, and rock and soul. From the background of its later developments the blues occasionally filters through as it once was, a soliloquy, a solo lament accompanied by mouth organ, piano or guitar. Centred on unrequited love and social subjugation, blues lyrics are not without moments of humour, aggression, irony and sexual allusions.

By far the most cultivated blues verse is the beautifully symmetrical twelve-bar structure divided into a three-part stanza: a vocal line is stated, reiterated and then concluded with a third line. Tense and laconic, the twelve-bar verse affords spacious intermissions for instrumental breaks. Epitomised in the songs and instrumental numbers of Big Bill Broonzy (1893–1958), W.C. Handy (1873–1958) and Huddy 'Leadbelly' Ledbetter (1885–1949), to name but three late exponents of the blues, the twelve-bar blues progression unwinds as Ex.137.

Ex. 137

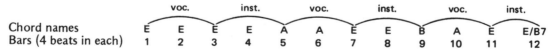

	voc.		inst.		voc.		inst.		voc.		inst.
Chord names	E	E	E	E	A	A	E	E	B	A	E	E/B7
Bars (4 beats in each)	1	2	3	4	5	6	7	8	9	10	11	12

After an optional introduction the twelve-bar cycle begins with a vocal statement varying in length from two to four bars on the tonic chord (Emajor, Ex.137). An instrumental break follows leading to the subdominant chord (Amajor, bars 5 and 6). The lyrics from the first line are repeated over these bars, but the melody is modified to suit its subdominant harmony. A plagal cadence to the tonic chord marks the start of the second instrumental break across the seventh and eighth bars. After a third concluding vocal line (bars 9 to 11) yet another instrumental break brings the verse to an end, in this case with a dominant 7th (B7) in anticipation of the next twelve-bar cycle.

Depending on the time allocated to the instrumental breaks, they can vary from curt or embellished arpeggios to decorated passages running into or flowing alongside the vocal lines. The scale basis for the vocal and instrumental figurations is a modified major, as often as not tinged with two 'blue' notes, the lowered 3rd and 7th degrees (Ex.138).

Ex. 138

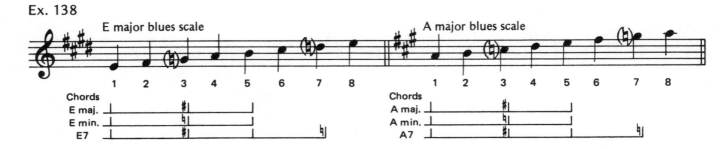

Reflecting the blues singer's emotional off-key delivery, the instrumental lines fluctutate between true and blue pitch. Tinted with these blue notes, the tonal shades of the harmony waver accordingly. If the lowered 3rd in the scale of E major occurs in the tonic chord it will convert that chord's quality from major (E, G sharp, B) to minor (E, G, B).

Ex. 139 12-bar blues variation on Ex. 137

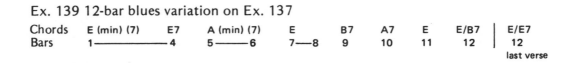

Chords	E (min) (7)		E7	A (min) (7)		E	B7	A7	E	E/B7	E/E7
Bars	1————		4	5———	6	7—8	9	10	11	12	12
											last verse

Moreover, the natural 7th (D) can be added to the tonic major particularly in the fourth bar where the conversion to a tonic 7th chord will effect a smooth transition to the subdominant chord (E7-A, Ex.139). Similarly the subdominant harmony will waver between Amajor, Aminor and A7 by interspersing blue notes from the scale of A major (bars 5-6). The very last verse often ends with an idiomatic blues tag, the tonic 7th (E7) instead of the concord, Emajor.

Ex. 140 'Walking' bass blues progression

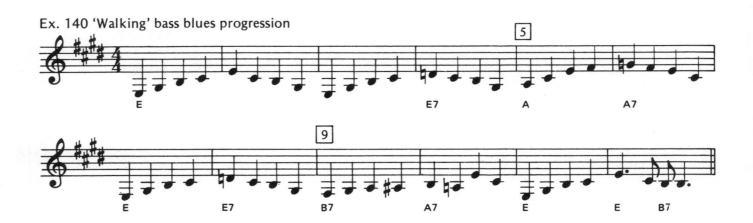

Ex. 141 Jumping beans
Sprightly

James Down

*play quaver pairs as 𝅘𝅥𝅭 𝅘𝅥𝅮 = 𝅘𝅥𝅮𝅘𝅥𝅮𝅘𝅥𝅮

A lighter side to the blues, the melodic pattern springing from the first bar of Ex.141 rebounds through the next two bars completing the opening statement on the tonic chord, Emajor. With the entry of D natural in bar 4 the tonic concord is changed to a tonic 7th. Keeping to the standard twelve-bar progression, bars 5 and 6 are centred on the subdominant, which in this instance is tinted with a flattened 7th scale note in A major (G), and ornamented with an added-note B. Returning to the opening statement in bar 7, the harmony then deviates from the standard progression: E7 replaces Emajor in bar 8, and in bar 9 Amajor takes two beats of what would normally be a four-beat bar of B7. For the last two bars a cute blues cliche is used. Rather than bide its time on the tonic chord, the melody is sidetracked through a descending 'turnaround' — where each step of the line is accompanied with a different chord. At the end of the turnaround the dominant chord is placed so as to anticipate the return of the tonic for the beginning of the next verse.

Lodged in a progression or even poised in isolation, a dominant 7th points predictably to its most likely resolution — and that doesn't altogether speak in its favour. Though a discord, its sting has long since gone from its tail. In folk song accompaniments the dominant 7th has become so mundane that it could well defer to other contenders — the diminished chord, for example, or one of its other substitutes that will present themselves in due course. Imposed in modal harmony a dominant 7th can sound conspicuously out of place. Its assertive tendency, associated more with major and minor harmony, is liable to run counter to modal lines whereas a dominant concord would not.

Not forgetting its positive sides, it is the dominant 7th which gives blues harmony its idiomatic colour, and the 7th note which generates extra impetus in popular song accompaniments. Finally, that 7th note ensures a keener grasp in a concluding cadence and directs the harmony to a new key chord in *modulation.*

8: MODULATION AND THE DIMINISHED 7th CHORD

Modulation

One of the richest sources of variety is attained through modulation — the movement between keys. When music modulates it abandons one key chord and centres on another, discarding notes from its former scale foundation and adopting others from the new found key. It may venture gradually from its home key and linger in one nearby with which it has notes in common; or jump restlessly through a host of distantly related key chords before finally returning to its point of departure.

Modulations may take place imperceptibly, or they can be sudden and marked. Smooth, unhurried modulations often indicate beforehand that a change of key is in the air. In preparation, the melody or harmony size up the prospective new key by absorbing its leading-note a bar or so ahead of the forthcoming keynote or chord. On other occasions they may seize the leading-note unexpectedly in passing and swivel on that into the new key centre.

Enticed or urged, modulation broadens the melodic and harmonic scope of a composition, it offers contrasts of mood. Of those chords that facilitate access to new keys, the dominant 7th is particularly important. Heralding the exit of the old key it beckons the next one in by announcing its leading-note and dominant with a full close introduction.

Ex. 142a   Ex. 142b

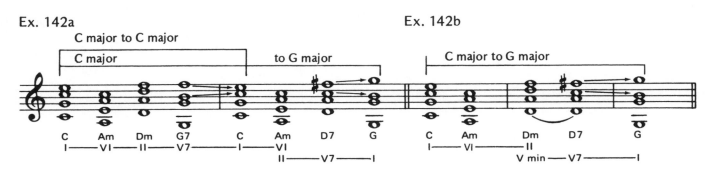

From its home key C major established by a full close, G7-Cmajor, Ex.142a then modulates to the dominant key G major. While the progression does not dilly-dally in its movements, it gives no impression of being forced out of one key and into the next. Two chords ensure a smooth transition. The first of these is Aminor in bar 2, a bridging chord common to the key of C major (V1), and G major (II). On this chord, a half-way point, the harmony has the option of returning to its home base or moving as it does through II-V7-I in root position to the key chord Gmajor. The second and most active chord in the modulation is the dominant 7th of the new key. This clinches the modulation by introducing the leading note and dominant of G major. The upper line with the leading-note, F sharp, rises and C immediately beneath, falls to resolve the tritone by contrary motion. Notice also the strong bass line leaping resolutely in 4ths from A to D then D to G, the root of the new key chord.

With no bridging chord, but just as smooth, Ex.142b modulates from C major to G major through the simple conversion of Dminor to D7. Arpeggiated and with passing notes added, an elaborated version of this progression occurs in bar 3 of Ex.143.

Ex. 143 Müss Ich Denn (cont'd from Ex. 28a)

Dm	Dm	C	C	Dm	D7		G
IIb	II	I	Ib	II	V7	of	I

C	Dm	C	C	Dm	G		C
I	II	I	I	II	Vb		I

Over a repeated bass note D, the middle voice in bar 3 steps upwards through F sharp while the upper line supplies C and A, converting Dminor to D7. But with so little time to establish itself, Gmajor is denied further claim to its newly acquired status as a tonic chord. Consequently it reverts to its original role, the dominant for a full close in C major.

Related keys

Each key has its own group of closely related keys. Modulations in standard harmony, particularly those in beginners pieces, take place between these keys. Concentrating for the present on modulations to related keys, they are the keys which differ from the home key by one sharp, flat or natural. The modulations just discussed were from C major to its closely related key, the dominant G major (with one sharp). Other closely related keys to C major are the subdominant F major (one flat); the relative minor, A minor, and the supertonic D minor (Ex.144).

Ex. 144

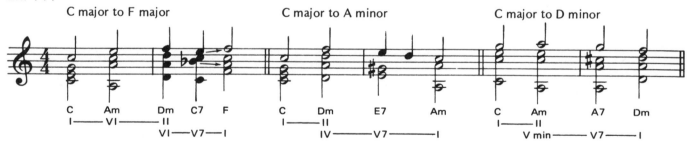

C major to F major				C major to A minor				C major to D minor			
C	Am	Dm	C7	F	C	Dm	E7	Am	C	Am	A7	Dm
I	VI	II			I	II			I	II		
		VI	V7	I		IV	V7	I			V min	V7	I

The home key, the point of departure for the music, is usually its eventual destination too. Key changes that occur between these points are passing or *transitory*. Often these so-called transitory modulations are not so much key changes in the true sense as intermediate cadences in keys outside the initial one. The examples given so far illustrate no more than the approaches to new key chords. Whether or not these approaches are exploited, meaning that they are followed up by a definite change of key, depends on other factors. If the melody and harmony do no more than strike a new key chord and quit it immediately without breaking momentum, they have not effected a conclusive modulation. In other words, they have gone through the motions of a modulation but have not endorsed it. When the lines land solidly on the new tonic via V, V7 or VII, and consolidate their new ground with a reiterated full close, then a definite modulation has taken place.

Demonstrating the difference between the merest transitory shift and a real modulation, Ex.145 embarks from its home key C major, touches on the supertonic D minor in passing, then later moves into the relative minor, A minor.

Ex. 145

In four sections defined by repeat signs, the first two sections in C major are balanced and contrasted by the following two in the relative minor.   Keeping to C major until bar 13, the melody then introduces C sharp, the leading-note for the prospective keynote D, and the bass provides its dominant A.   D minor is duly stated but is too short-lived to be regarded as a new key centre.   So rather than prompt a modulation, C sharp acts more as a chromatic embellishment in the melody.

Though the third section (from bar 17) begins with the chord A minor, the key of A minor is not established until its envoy E7, bars 18-19, confirms it.   From there to the end of the fourth section the leading-note bobs up every so often holding the melody and bass to their new found anchor A.   So settled has the music become in this key that it could well end there; but the old one, C major, is reinstated by the postscript D.C. (Da Capo), meaning that the opening section should be repeated to the word 'fine'.

Minor key modulations

Modulations in minor keys are generally to the relative major and subdominant (Ex.146).

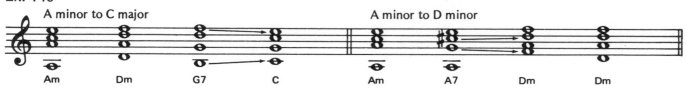

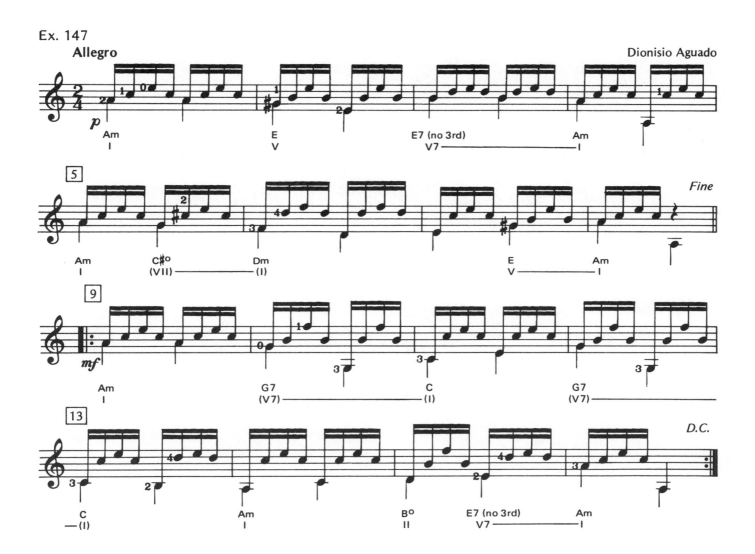

Once again, a composition that has a fleeting modulation followed by a sustained one. From its home key A minor established over the first four bars, Ex.147 is then manoeuvred through C sharp diminished in bar 5 to a transitory new key chord, the subdominant Dminor. Moving to bar 10, a definite modulation takes place to the relative major. The first indication of this is the entry of G natural in the bass (as opposed to G sharp) and the 7th of G7 in the melody. From this chord the leading-note B rises to the keynote C in the new tonic chord. Affirming the modulation is another V-I progression over bars 12 and 13. Returning to the initial key, the bass descends by step from C to A, the root of Aminor which is re-established by a full close in the home key.

Modulation in other major and minor keys

Ex. 148

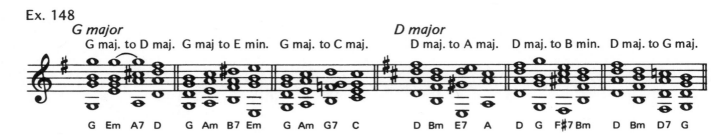

Ex. 149 Minuet. G major (cont'd from Ex. 97)

J. S. Bach

From its home key G major, Ex.149 cautiously prepares a modulation to D major by first announcing that key's leading-note no less than four bars ahead of the key chord in bar 24. And yet after such a calculated approach, D major is immediately annulled by the bass line which steps through C natural thereby cancelling the foregoing sharps. Though Dmajor does pop up before the section is through, it is strictly as a dominant since there is no C sharp in its vicinity to qualify it as a potential key chord.

Ex. 150 Lullaby (A major)

H. Martinez

Unashamedly romantic and with a Mexican folk-like flavour to it, the first phrase of Ex.150 is centred mainly on the tonic chord, and to balance this, the second phrase, on the dominant chord, ends with a full close. At the beginning of the third phrase G natural completes A7 which edges the harmony into the subdominant key, D major. Now while this passing tonic chord has a whole bar in which to find its feet, the melody still bears allegiance to its initial key. With G sharp retained in the ascending line (bar 13), the key of A major with a G sharp note prevails over D major with its G natural note.

Incidentally, the augmented chord explained in 110b appears twice here, now as F sharp augmented (bars 18 and 27). In this case it is F sharp major — F sharp, A sharp with its upper note (C sharp) raised a semitone. Hence its augmented 5th is F sharp to C double-sharp or D. As illustrated in Ex.110b, one note of the augmented interval is placed in the upper line, and the other in the bass. Momentarily tautened by this dissonance the harmony is then relaxed by the fall of the melody to C sharp, completing the concord F sharp major.

Another important detail is the sequence of bass notes across bars 27 and 28. These progress with perfect 4ths, F sharp-B-E-A. The major/minor chord progression arising from this bass line will, if pursued in leaps of a 4th, turn full circle (Ex.151).

Ex. 151

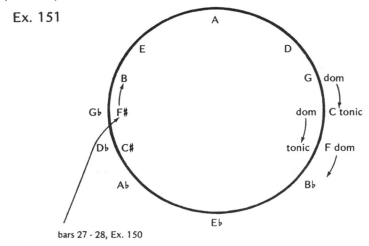

bars 27 - 28, Ex. 150

Besides bass lines, this 4th sequence has been a versatile resource for the development of chord progressions and melodic patterning. In these roles it has occurred in many guises over several centuries. In particular, it is ubiquitous in Baroque music, the 18th-century dance suites of Bach and Handel, wherein it arises as sequential patterns spun from actual or implied chord progressions a 4th apart: A-D-G, etc. As such the part-weaving from this cycle emerges either as chordal arpeggiations or in contrapuntal sequences in the manner of Ex.150.

Nicknamed 'round the clock' by jazz musicians, the tonic-dominant-tonic sequence in Ex.151 serves as a pattern for brief or extended bass lines underlying major, minor and dominant 7th chord accompaniments for jazz evergreens and popular songs. Apart from being a firm harmonic progression, chord movements in perfect 4ths facilitate modulations to remote keys. A verse of a song may end in its home key, say G major, then after a bridge progression, Gmajor-C7-F7, the accompaniment for the next verse may begin in the key of B flat major via the full close F7-B flat.

Tracing the circle anticlockwise (G-D-A), its notes are spaced in perfect 5ths, the *circle of 5ths*. Regarding these notes as the roots of key chords, then the key signatures for those key chords gain an additional sharp with each forward leap: G major (one sharp), D major (two sharps), etc. Through the spectrum of flat keys, they lose a flat with each anticlockwise move: E flat major (three flats), B flat major (two flats).

So the circle of 5ths shows what modulations will lead to progressively sharper keys: G major, D major, A major; and progressively flatter keys: F major, B flat major, E flat major. To conduct these modulations refer to Ex.148, transposing for those keys not given, and to another chord waiting to take part in modulation, the *diminished 7th*.

The diminished 7th chord

At home in the harmony of Bach or the blues, the versatile and ambiguous *diminished 7th* may be inset into a progression simply as a colouring device, or like the dominant 7th, to conduct a modulation. But unlike the dominant 7th which is pledged to particular major and minor resolutions, the chameleon-like diminished 7th will merge with a variety of near and distantly related chords.

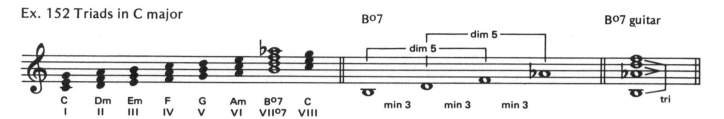

Ex. 152 Triads in C major

The diminished chord in Ex.152 is the diminished traid, Bdiminished, with an additional 7th note A flat. Ascending in equidistant intervals of a minor 3rd, its two overlapping tritones long to resolve, yet give little indication as to how this will take place. Though by virtue of its ambiguity, a diminished 7th has various outlets for resolution, often those major and minor chords whose bass notes are a step away from the bass of the diminished 7th (Ex.153).

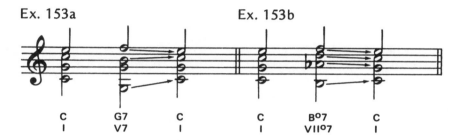

Ex. 153a   Ex. 153b

Where in the full close (Ex.153a), one voice is stationary, G-G, Ex.153b is more decisive because all of its voice parts contribute to the resolution. Furthermore, as both progressions have the same upper line, the latter may be considered as a substitute for the overworked dominant 7th in the full close. Remember that the letter name for the diminished 7th substitute is the same as the leading note for the tonic chord in question B dim7-C major.

The diminished 7th in the minor key

Corresponding with the diminished 7th in C major, the diminished 7th equivalent in the relative minor is VII with a 7th note, a minor 3rd above D (Ex.154).

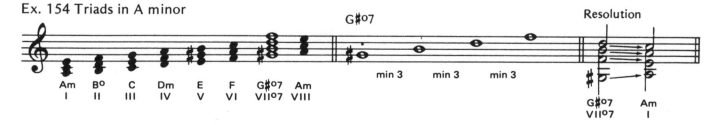

Ex. 154 Triads in A minor

Ex. 155 Study in C major

F. Sor
etc.

Underpinned by a pedal bass C, the melody and its fluctuating middle line are centred first on the tonic chord then veer in bar 3 to the implied dominant 7th, G7, and return to the tonic for the fourth bar. Later in the study, (from bar 25), the melody from the opening four bars is repeated but its harmony is varied by a transition from the home key C major via G sharp dim7 to the relative minor, A minor.

Given a repeated melody, how can its harmony be varied in the way that this is, by a change of key? First decide what the new chord will be, then how it might be approached. Whatever the prospective key chord is, it must contain the relevant melody notes. Sor has opted for the relative minor chord which both contains the original melody note (C in the second half of bar 4), and offers a minor shade to contrast the earlier major. To conduct the modulation, one note from the melody has been singled out and on that a bridging chord is placed. In this instance it the melody note D, formally a suspension on Cmajor and now the upper note of G sharp dim7. Equally, this could have been the 7th note D in E7, which in 2nd inversion would allow the bass to descend by step from C through B to A: Cmajor-E7-Aminor.

A diminished 7th may be inserted between two unrelated chords as a bridge for modulation, or as matchmaker, bind them as part of a continuous progression without any suggestion of a modulation. Then again, with quite the opposite effect, this versatile chord is likely to rear up from an unexpected quarter, arresting the harmony or diverting it along a new track. Before the diminished 7th is demonstrated in these roles, there are some curious facets of its makeup to consider: for depending on which of its four notes lies in the bass it can be called by one of four different letter names.

Ex. 156a   Ex. 156b   Ex. 156c

Three different arrangements of the same notes, Ex.156a is the chord just dealt with, Bdim7. From its bass B the chord receives its letter name. Rearranging these notes as Ex.156b, this formation also ascends in minor 3rds so it too is a diminished 7th chord. To illustrate the interval layout common to both formations, the note B from Ex.156a is *enharmonically changed* to C flat in Ex.156b. Enharmonic change means changing the name of a note but not its pitch. With a bass D, Ex.156b is called Ddim7. In practice this might be notated as Ex.156c, where C flat reverts to B.

Ex. 157a   Ex. 157b   Ex. 157c

Rearranging the four notes twice again, Ex.157a has minor 3rds ascending from F through A flat to C flat then E double-flat (hitherto D natural). Practical notation for these notes is shown in Ex.157b. To clarify the minor 3rd ascendancy in Ex.157c, A flat is enharmonically changed to G sharp. This, like the other formations, derives its letter name from its bass note. Despite their individual letter names, Exs.156 and 157 have in common a *characteristic sound:* that of a diminished 7th comprising four specific notes — B, D, F, A flat (EX.158).

Ex. 158

As Bdim7 has the same characteristic sound as its companion diminished 7ths, Ddim7, Fdim7 and A flat dim7, then one or all four of these chords can be used to substitute G7. Moreover, each formation performs an individual function, leaning towards, and so emphasising, the chord next to it (Ex.159).

Ex. 159 Sonato Eroica opus 150

Sidling into the sixth bar of Ex.159, the diminished 7th draws attention not to itself despite its stress on an accented beat, but to the adjoining chord F sharp minor. The purpose of the diminished 7th here is not to summon a new key by acting as a substitute for a dominant 7th, but to add a dissonant relish to its concordant surrounding, and motion the melody gently up one step after its sudden drop from F sharp.

Resolved decisively in contrary motion, this diminished 7th is simply a harmonic embellishment, a passing discord projecting the following concord without stemming the flow of the lines. With the opposite effect, the diminished 7th in Ex.160 stops the harmony in mid-air so as to prevent the phrase from ending prematurely.

Ex. 160

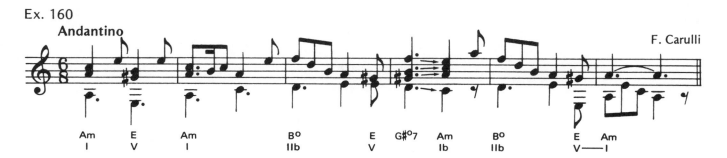

Springing up from behind the dominant chord, the diminished 7th in the fourth bar arrests the melody and bass line, and in doing so, diverts them from a full close which at this juncture would have curtailed the phrase half way through. Held momentarily in abeyance, the lines then fall to an inconclusive tonic chord which allows them the opportunity to retrace their foregoing steps and follow these through to a conclusive ending in a root position full close.

Ex. 161

Diminished 7th scale

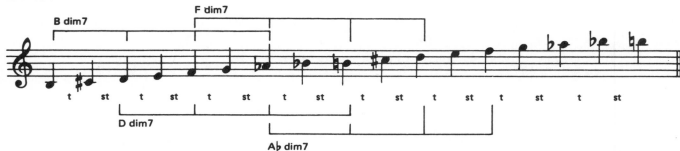

A synthetic scale derived from the diminished 7th chord is as unique in character and sound as the chord itself. Progressing in alternating tones and semitones, its 1st, 3rd, 5th and 7th degrees are the notes of Bdim7; and those in Ddim7, Fdim7 and A flat dim7 follow the same sequence in the scale but from their respective bass notes.

Melodic improvisations on Bdim7 (or G7) can be sketched with the range of notes from B to A flat in the scale, or if time permits, extended across its full compass. The same source of notes would be used for improvisations on Ddim7, Fdim7 and A flat dim7, beginning on the respective bass notes.

Of course, it isn't necessary to channel improvisations around a predetermined chord progression. Time spent on indeterminate improvisation will eventually repay with a promising idea. A melody based on this scale and an awaiting harmony of four diminished 7th chords will surely be novel in design and dissonant in sound.

Other diminished 7th chords

Between them, three diminished 7th chords contain every sharp, flat and natural note. Dividing the octave into semitone steps, the *chromatic* scale, we shall see which of these notes are contained in the three diminished 7ths (Ex.162).

Ex. 162 Chromatic scale on B

Four notes, B, D, F, A flat (G sharp) from the chromatic scale have already been taken care of in Bdim7 and its related formations. The other scale notes are accommodated by one or the other of the chords in Exs.163.

Ex. 163a   Ex. 163b

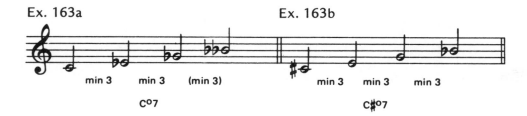

Depending on which of its notes is the bass, Ex.163a may have one of four letter names. From being Cdim7, its notes may be rearranged and enharmonically changed as E flat (D sharp), G flat (F sharp) or Adim7. Similarly Ex.163b as C sharp dim7, Edim7, etc.

Ex. 164 Major and diminished 7th chord chain

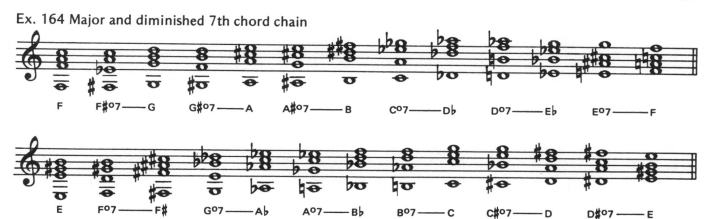

Two cycles of alternating concords and discords, Ex.164 contains all the diminished 7ths given, now arranged for the guitar with major chord resolutions. Besides majors, the resolving chords can be minors or major/minor inversions provided that their bass notes are those shown.

Links may be extracted from the chain and utilised in the following ways: first as substitute progressions for full close cadences; instead of D7-G major, try F sharp dim7-Gmajor (where the letter name of the diminished 7th is the same as the leading-note for the chord in question). Secondly, as bridging chords for modulation between keys with tonic chords a tone apart. For example, should you wish to lift the key for a verse of a song up one tone from say G major to A major, then G sharp dim7 will bridge those key chords, e.g. Gmajor-G sharp dim7-Amajor.

Also from the cycle but modified to suit a descending melody, Ex.165 has three diminished 7ths with their resolving major chords in a roundabout and embellished modulation from A minor to C major.

Ex. 165 Study in A minor

Descending in *sequences*, the harmonic pattern of D sharp dim7 and its resolving major is imitated a tone lower as C sharp dim7 to D major, and again as Bdim7 to Cmajor. In spite of the bass line's assertive upward steps (potential leading-notes to passing key chords), the sheer weight and momentum behind the descending lines prevents them from taking root on their major chords. A notable harmonisation, its snappy alternations of tension and release produce a chequered harmonic texture, while at the same time directing the lines downwards to taper off with a cadential $^6_4$ $^5_3$ in the relative major key.

Diminished 7th embellishing primary chord progressions

If I-IV-V are the principal chords for a song accompaniment, chances are that they will occur with some persistency. To avoid the drudgery of their repetition, vary the accompaniment with I-VI-II-V as suggested in Exs.61, and the other alternative progression in Ex.166.

Ex. 166 Primary chords in C major

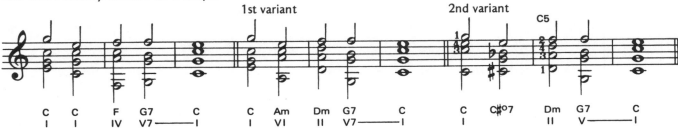

Ex. 167

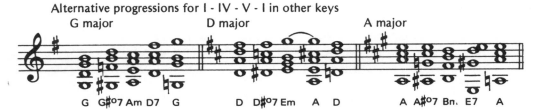

Diminished 7ths to dominant 7ths

Diminished 7ths are not always resolved by major/minor chords, nor indeed is their resolution obligatory. Placed in front of a dominant 7th they will enhance the approach to that chord either during the course of a progression or in a full or half close (Ex.168).

Ex. 168 Diminished 7ths to dominant 7ths

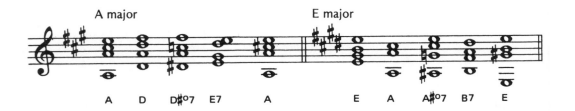

Within the various contexts in which the diminished 7th has appeared, only once did its resolution urge the harmony to rest: in a substitute progression for a full close. Apart from that it nestled in where, depending on the effect required, it either boosted the harmony on its way, or arrested it in mid-course. Possessing a potential leading-note, a diminished 7th will also effect a modulation between two seemingly unrelated keys.

Where the diminished 7th paid court to a chord other than the tonic of the key it was not allocated with a Roman numeral (except as II in minor keys). Numbers signify the disposition of chord roots in relation to the presiding tonic, i.e. I-IV-V, C-F-G, where the numerals denote the progression of the triads' roots in relation to their keynote C. Most of the diminished 7ths here, however, were *chromatic* adjuncts, meaning that they were not component chords of the diatonic structures housing them. Therefore they were assessed in a particular connection, that is, in relation to their adjoining chords. In this respect they were distinguished from diatonic chords which related back to their tonics. Nevertheless, as an aid to analysis or for transposition, chromatic chords can sometimes be denoted with numerals. For example, Cmajor-Fmajor-F sharp dim7-G could be denoted as I-IV-#IVdim7-V. A transposition of this progression to the key of G major is then conducted in terms of its symbols: I-IV-#IVdim7-V or Gmajor Cmajor-C sharp dim7-D.

Another chromatic chord just as mobile and ambiguous in sound is the *augmented 6th*. This, like the diminished 7th, performs two functions: it bonds two unrelated chords within the course of a progression, or as a bridging chord, conducts a modulation between them (Ex.169).

Ex. 169

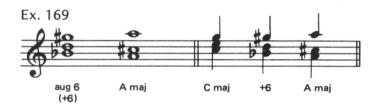

aug 6   A maj   C maj   +6   A maj
(+6)

Called the *Italian 6th* to distinguish it from other types of augmented 6th chords, Ex.169 has as its outer interval an augmented 6th, B flat-G sharp. This is a semitone bigger than a major 6th (B flat-G, see also Ex.39b).

While readily adapting to diatonic harmony, an augmented 6th chord, like a diminished 7th, is nevertheless a chromatic passing chord. Therefore it is not numerically labelled since that would signify a root relationship with the parent tonic. What stands out clearly in Ex.169 is three adjacent voice parts 'pulled' by the augmented 6th in contrary motion to their resolution, the concordant interval in Amajor. That is the way to regard the chord: horizontally and not as a vertical note column at so many degrees from the principal tonic.

Ex. 170 Study in A minor

F. Sor

C   aug 6 —— A   C#°—— Dm   aug 6 —— G   B°—— C   E7—— Am   Em   Dm sus   Dm   E
                                                                              V♮3   IV   V

Where the phrase in Ex.165 has diminished 7ths and major chords in four-part harmony, its continuation here is reduced by one part to three-note augmented 6ths and major chords. A subtle contrast is achieved between the former phrase with its denser harmony and descending melody, and this, a lighter harmony with an undulating melody. In these respects the two phrases differ; yet they also bear a marked similarity: here too identical patterns or sequences occur in one-tone intervals. The first is an augmented 6th with its resolution Amajor and the second is the augmented 6th with Gmajor.

Against those strictly diatonic progressions outlined some chapters back, these with a liberal infusion of chromatic notes, are considerably more colourful. Though not disrupting the overall balance of the diatonic structure containing them, the diminished 7th and augmented 6th did inevitably relegate the principal key chord to the background by drawing subordinate harmonies momentarily into the limelight. No longer had the tonic chord exclusive right to a leading-note to herald its arrival: and no longer had it solely diatonic chords rallying round. Both the diminished 7th and augmented 6th possess potential leading-notes, and directed by these, the harmony could rest at, or pass through, a variety of key chords far removed from its initial key centre.

Broadening major and minor harmony upwards as well as outwards, melody notes over and above 7ths will next be added to three-note triads, enlarging them as *extended chords*.

9: EXTENDED CHORDS

Free a melody from its harmony, and both will benefit from the exercise. Given the rein, the melody can leap ahead, trail behind and reach for notes outside those prescribed by its accompanying chords. And the harmony gains too from the melody's caprices. By absorbing the errant melody notes, the chords expand with new adornments.

In this way the dominant chord grew in size and standing. Accepting its 7th as an integral part, that chord acquired an additional force to intensify its drive. Similarly, by displacing one note within a gathering of melodies produced a suspension which both invigorated the chord containing it and boosted the rhythm.

When 7ths and suspensions are applied without reservation and are allowed to compete with their accompanying chord notes in terms of duration and stress, they will be heard not as passing decorations but as harmonic enrichments. It needs only to relax the old practice of preparing and resolving embellishments, and new chords will emerge as extensions of their former selves. This uninhibited treatment of melody and harmony accelerated over the second half of the 19th century. Unrestrained melodic overlays on standard progressions gradually converted common chords into complex extensions. Though their proliferation was stumped in the early 20th century by altogether new theoretical tactics it continued to make headway into jazz. Before working round to the use of extended chords in this field there is one device to cover that had much to do with their evolution, the *appoggiatura*.

Ex. 171

G Am D7 G

Literally the appoggiatura means a 'leaning' note, an additional note tied to a chord as a decoration. The appoggiatura in Ex.171 is the note B over the dominant 7th. This discord is intensified by the clash of its appoggiatura with C in the chord (C-B, a major 7th). In this case the dissonance is stressed, falling on an accented beat. Leaning in the direction of its intended resolution, the melody steps down to A, relieving its host chord of one of its dissonances.

The significance of the appoggiatura is far greater than a freely applied decoration. Its dissonant potential and the downward inclination it exerts on a melody proved to be a highly expressive force in 19th century orchestral and operatic music. Wagner and Liszt, in particular, used appoggiature to convey yearning, anguish and other dramatic effects that characterised the 'romantic' movement in music at that time. Laced freely into the harmony and often without resolution, appoggiaturas were soon accepted as component notes of the chords, effectively augmenting them. Not limited to diatonic additions, the harmonic advances in the late 19th century yielded an abundance of chromatic additions and complete chromatic passing chords. Out-numbering or at least equalling their diatonic constituents, these rich and complex chords extended Western harmony from its former diatonic foundations into an expanse of chromaticism.

Returning to the appoggiatura in its basic form, it differs from a traditional suspension in that it can enter the harmony from any angle, without preparation from the previous chord (Ex.172).

Ex. 172   M. Carcassi

After an opening arpéggio Amajor, the first appoggiatura enters as F sharp in the upper line which falls to E, an essential note of its accompanying chord. The melodic interest is then switched to the bass which echoes the preceding downward step by its descent from A to G sharp. Under the same appoggiatura, the harmony changes in bar 2 to G sharp diminished (not G sharp dim7 because the upper interval D-F sharp is a major 3rd). The fall of the melody from this appoggiatura completes E7 in 1st inversion. Carried into bar 3, E7 awaits the third appoggiatura that now arises as a blatant *unprepared* suspension. Unannounced, this appoggiatura is nevertheless resolved by the downward step of the melody to G sharp, restoring E7 in full. Over the tonic chord in bar 4 the appoggiatura B creates a combined dissonance, a major 2nd, A-B and a minor 7th, C sharp-B. Of the two melody notes in bar 5, the first is active, A-G sharp, a major 7th, but the second F sharp is not disruptive since the 5th of the chord (E) is not there to object. In bar 6 the resolution of the suspension F sharp to E completes A sharp dim7, steering the harmony to B7 (see also Ex.168). With its prepared suspension resolved, B7 is then ready to summon a modulation to E major.

Appoggiature embellish their chords in one or two ways. Ex.172 shows both of these. As oblique melodic decorations they ornament a chord progression which in plain form is self-contained. From this point of view, the appoggiature in Ex.172 are heard as melodic additions passing over a conventional progression of common chords. But this analysis does not take into account the fact that the appoggiature here are stressed and carry as much melodic weight as the other chord notes. Therefore they qualify as integral parts of extended chords. And that is just how they will sound if they are played together with their neighbouring notes as block chords. From this treatment sprang the 7th, 9th, 11th and 13th chords used in jazz.

Jazz progressions

Extended chords with 7ths and beyond abound in jazz harmony. Where they differ from the appoggiatura chords just described is not in content but presentation — with the spirit and rhythmic vitality of jazz. Though added-note chords are not exclusive to a particular jazz style, they flourished in the early forties to mid-fifties bebop movement. During this highly contrapuntal and harmonically exploratory epoch of American jazz, numerous jazz 'clichés', that is, embellished cadences and chordal paraphrases for basic progressions, were fashioned. Some of these have passed out of fashion and now sound merely nostalgic, but many others have not only survived but thrive anew in the jazz guitars of the old timers Tal Farlow, Barney Kessel and Joe Pass plus comparative newcomers, John Abercrombie, Louis Stewart, from a host of leading names, not to mention the incalculable contributions from jazz pianists.

If embellishments are not specified in a jazz accompaniment, the guitarist or pianist adds his extensions and alterations to basic chords. For example, the chord Gmajor would be coloured with one, or possibly three, additional notes sounded successively or in combination. Each decoration imbues the chord with a different tonal shade, some akin in sound to Gmajor, others the vaguest reflection of it. Foremost among these decorations are 7ths. Once they have been added to major and minor chords others will follow, above these notes or in place of them.

Ex. 173

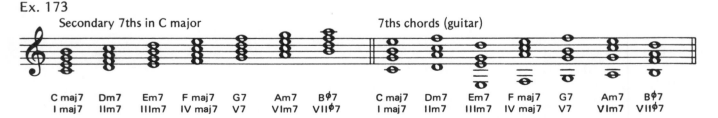

| C maj7 | Dm7 | Em7 | F maj7 | G7 | Am7 | Bø7 | C maj7 | Dm7 | Em7 | F maj7 | G7 | Am7 | Bø7 |
| I maj7 | IIm7 | IIIm7 | IV maj7 | V7 | VIm7 | VIIø7 | I maj7 | IIm7 | IIIm7 | IV maj7 | V7 | VIm7 | VIIø7 |

When a 7th is added to a dominant triad, its sound changes from a concord to a disgruntled discord. Not so the other chords in Ex.173; though they are discords too, their 7ths give them extra colour without obscuring their major/minor qualities. All except G7 are *secondary* 7th chords, so called to distinguish them from V, the principal (dominant) 7th chord in the key. Do not confuse the term secondary in this context with secondary triads II, III, VI and VII in a major and minor key.

Regarding the tonic chord, this has a 7th note B, a major 3rd above G. Sometimes major 7th chords are denoted with a capital M, hence CM7 In either case, the symbol 'maj' or M refers to the major quality of the chord and not to the distance of its outer notes (C-B, a major 7th). Similarly, the symbol Dmin7 or Dm7 denotes a minor triad with an added 7th, without specific reference to the outer interval (D-C, a minor 7th). The chord VII7 is a *half-diminished 7th* (B diminished plus A, symbol Bⵁ 7). To qualify as a 'full' diminished 7th its upper interval must be a minor 3rd (Bdim7 — B, D, F, A flat). Sometimes this secondary 7th is analysed as Bmin7 (B, D, F sharp, A) with its 5th flattened (B, D, F, A, denoted Bm7-5). Strictly speaking this definition is technically incorrect since to qualify as a minor triad, the chord should have a perfect 5th (B-F sharp). Even so, flattened 5th symbols are rife in jazz scores and that fully justifies their inclusion here.

Style permitting, secondary 7ths can replace basic triad type progressions. For instance, I-VI-II-V-I dressed up as Cmaj7-Amin7-Dmin7-G7 in two-beat changes are the chords for choruses in 'Blue Moon', 'These Foolish Things' and numerous other jazz standards. Apart from embellishing the progressions outlined in Chapter Three, secondary 7ths may also be set along novel lines for song accompaniments or instrumental pieces (Ex.174).

Ex. 174 Secondary 7ths in C major

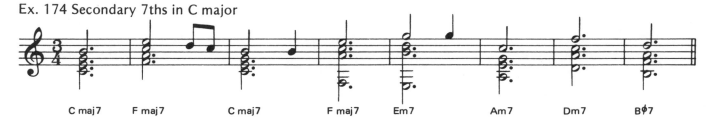

C maj7   F maj7   C maj7   F maj7   Em7   Am7   Dm7   Bⵁ7

There is much to be said for placing the chords in any order just to see what turns up. And as most shapes leave one or two fingers free, those not engaged stopping chord notes can weave a melody in and around the chord changes.

Against the subtle tints of secondary 7ths, the dominant 7th stands out like a sore thumb. Consider instead the half-diminished 7th which contains the essential element of the dominant 7th (the tritone F-B) but blends much better with the other chords. Moreover, because of its ambiguous quality, this chord is not totally committed to the tonic and will therefore act as a bridge to the relative minor (Ex.175).

Ex. 175

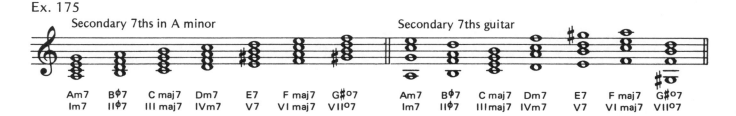

Secondary 7ths in A minor

Am7   Bⵁ7   C maj7   Dm7   E7   F maj7   G♯°7
Im7   IIⵁ7   III maj7   IVm7   V7   VI maj7   VII°7

Secondary 7ths guitar

Am7   Bⵁ7   C maj7   Dm7   E7   F maj7   G♯°7
Im7   IIⵁ7   IIImaj7   IVm7   V7   VI maj7   VII°7

Chords I and IV in the minor key are minor 7ths, V is the dominant 7th and VII is a diminished 7th. Despite their comparative modernity, minor key secondary 7ths can at times substitute triad chords in the accompaniments of modal folk songs. They also support the melodies in modal jazz, a refined jazz strain that arose in the late fifties out of the heat of the bop torrent. Generally, modal jazz harmony is austere and reticent, allowing unrestricted scope for melodic invention based on the Aeolian or Dorian modes (Ex.176).

Ex. 176 Aeolian secondary 7ths

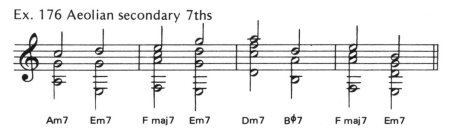

Am7   Em7   F maj7   Em7   Dm7   Bⵁ7   F maj7   Em7

Secondary 7ths can be built on any major, minor or modal scale and their progressions may follow standard sequences or take novel turns as those in Ex.174. Chord notes not directly participating in the melody, bass or supporting line could be weeded out either to lend starkness to the harmony or to make room for other additions, the 6th, 9th and 13th notes.

Chords with added 6ths, 7ths, 9ths and 13th notes

Combined with or taking the place of 7ths, added 6ths and 9ths decorate major and minor chords, and 9ths and 13ths decorate dominant 7ths. These embellishments are either stated specifically with the chord symbols or are left to the guitarist to add at will (Exs.177).

Ex. 177

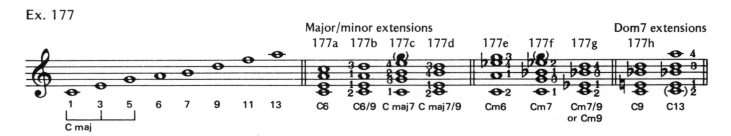

Ex.177a is a C major triad with its 5th (G) omitted and a 6th A added. Ex.177b has an added 6th plus a 9th D. Ex.177c is Cmaj7 and Ex.177d is Cmaj7 with a 9th. Ex.177e is a C minor triad with an added 6th A. Ex.177f is Cmin7 and Ex.177g is Cmin7 with its 5th omitted and a 9th D added. One or possibly all four of the major extensions could substitute a plain C major chord at a cadence or during the course of a progression. Likewise, Cmin6, Cmin7 and occasionally Cmin9 will substitute Cminor. For example, instead of a four-beat bar of the given chord Cmajor, play two beats of Cmaj7 followed by two beats of C6/9.

All shapes are moveable and when shifted to other positions they will adopt different letter names. At present C6/9, Cmaj7/9 and Cmin6 are at the second position where the first finger lies behind the second fret. Notice that their letter names are the same as their root notes, in each case the bass C. Shifted to 4th position (first finger behind the fourth fret) these chords will have a bass note D with letter names D6/9, Dmaj7/9 and Dmin6. At the 6th position their bass notes will be E, hence: E6/9, Emaj7/9, Emin6.

Ex.177h shows embellished dominant 7ths in the key of F major (C7-F). The first is C7 with an added 9th note D, and the second has a 9th plus a 13th A. This note is denoted as a 13th because it is added over the 7th in a dominant chord: C13 – C, E, (G), B flat plus the 13th A. In a non-dominant role such as C6 then A is the 6th: C6 – C, E, (G), A. To function as dominant chords they must include their 7ths but as dominant 13ths their 9ths can be omitted. As this 13th shape demands a left-hand stretch, its root may also be omitted. The absence of the root will not dilute the chord's strength for it still has a tritone (E-B flat) to endorse its dominant status. To distinguish dominant 7ths from secondary 7ths, a dominant 7th has no maj/min qualifying symbol (C9 not Cmaj9). Extensions of secondary major triads have 'maj' included in their symbols (except 6th and 6/9 chords).

Ex. 178

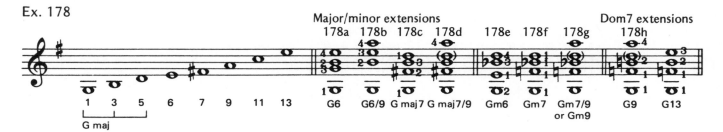

Exs.178 are again major, minor and dominant 7th extensions, but as different chord shapes cover another range of letter names. All are in root position and take their letter names from their bass notes. Shifted to 5th position (first finger barré behind fifth fret except Ex.178e), their letter names will be the same as their root notes, in each case A.

A progression of common major, minor and dominant 7th chords could be embellished in the following way (Ex.179).

Ex. 179

standard (std)	4/4	F	∕	∕	∕	Bb	∕	∕	∕	Eb7	∕	Ebm	∕	Ab	∕	Abm	∕
substitutes (subs)	4/4	F6	∕	F maj7	∕	Bb maj7	∕	Bb6/9	∕	Eb9	∕	Ebm7	∕	Ab maj7	∕	Abm7	∕

Under the given progression the substitutes in Ex.179 begin with F6, the chord shape in Ex.178a shifted to first position. Fmaj7 is Ex.178c at first position; B flat maj7 is Ex.177c at first position, also Ex.178c at 6th position. B flat6/9 could be Ex.177b shifted down two frets or Ex.178b at 6th position. E flat9 is Ex.177h in 5th position. E flat min7 is Ex.177f at 6th position. A flat maj7 is Ex.178c at 4th position and A flat min7 is Ex.178f also in 4th position.

Through *voice-leading* one or more melodic strands impart a discernible directional force. Notes within the chord progressions are aligned to weave horizontally as well as merge in vertical arrays. Should the upper melody line take priority in voice-leading, then where it draws on extended chord notes, 6ths, 9ths and so on, these are led to resolution usually by falling a step to essential, component notes of the chords. However, in jazz harmony, like other instrumental music, underlying voice parts in parallel with the outer melody may be interwoven too. In cases where the upper line is stationary, lower strands may be arranged to converge and separate. These parts too may include added chord notes, now embedded within the harmony.

Taking first an upper melody as the principal component of voice-leading, where it involves 9th and 13th notes, these may fall in resolution to the 5ths or roots of their chords (Ex.180a-b).

Ex. 180a   Ex. 180b   Ex. 180c

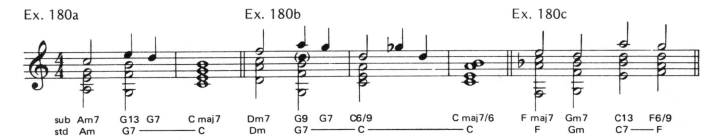

In Ex.180a the upper line with the appoggiatura E falls to D, the 5th of the dominant 7th chord. The appoggiatura 9th in Ex.180b falls to the octave root of the chord. Sometimes, and particuarly during fast tempos, 9th and 13th notes are not resolved separately as appoggiature but simultaneously with their chords as component notes (Ex.180c). Where the melody is not the leading part, a lower line maintains continuity either by remaining at the same pitch or moving in semitone steps (see Ex.181, the accompaniment for 'All The Things You Are', starting note B flat).

Ex. 181

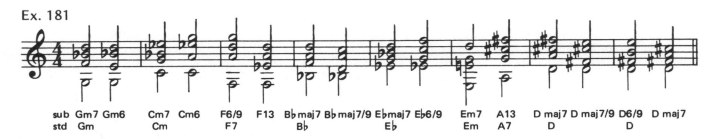

| sub | Gm7 | Gm6 | Cm7 | Cm6 | F6/9 | F13 | Bb maj7 | Bb maj7/9 | Ebmaj7 | Eb6/9 | Em7 | A13 | D maj7 | D maj7/9 | D6/9 | D maj7 |
| std | Gm | | Cm | | F7 | | Bb | | Eb | | Em | A7 | D | | D | |

The extended chords in Ex.181 are played at frets where their root bass notes are the same as the letter names for the given chords. Notes within the chords may be omitted or rearranged to improve the continuity of the upper line or inner parts. For example, Cmin7 in bar 2 could have its 5th G placed in the upper line rather than beneath it: Cmin7 — C, B flat, E flat, G, ascending in this order.

Given a vertical emphasis, this progression is a homophonic accompaniment for an instrumental or vocal line. In solo instrumental pieces the melody both plays close to its chords and ventures to their very brink. Aside from the 1st, 3rd and 5th notes of the chords, the melody can also reach out for 7ths, 9ths and 13ths and still roam within arms length of its harmony (Ex.182).

Ex. 182 Nuance

L.B.

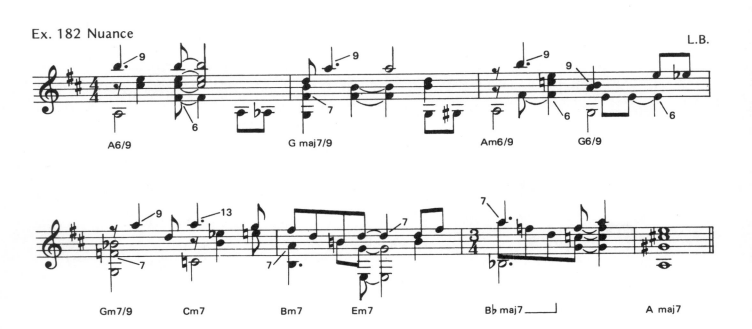

Jazz melodies are often projected with accented appoggiature. Not only do these enrich the overall sound, they lessen the dependence of the melody on the harmony. In Ex.182 the upper line was conceived as a series of added-notes with suitable chords structured around them. Equally, the melody could have been set by grafting 6ths, 7ths, 9ths or 13ths on a given basic chord progression. Where the melody is sustained or stops, the impetus is carried by other parts moving by step or spread as arpeggios. To these, further decorations and finer contrapuntal gradations can be obtained through the insertions of *altered-note chords.*

Suspensions, flattened 5th and flattened 9th substitutions

Only so many notes can be tacked to plain chords before they become so heavily laden as to be unmanageable. So rather than extend them further, alterations will next be made to their existing structures. By flattening certain notes within them, they emerge as malformations as well as extensions of their former selves. New discords result offering a wider range of harmonic variety. With chromatic alterations the chords become more pliable and can then be individually moulded to fit a particular niche in a progression. The first of these alterations is one already dealt with, a suspension in a dominant 7th. Coupled to this is another distortion of a dominant 7th, the *dominant 7th flattened 5th* (Ex.183).*

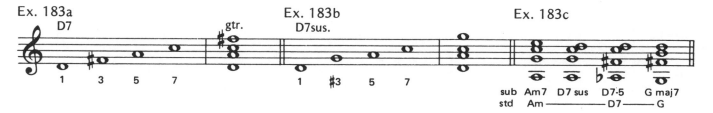

If the 3rd in Ex.183a is raised to G as Ex.183b, D7 is converted into D7 suspended. Arranged for the guitar, the suspension G in Ex.183c is prepared by the preceding chord, and the 5th of the dominant is placed in the bass. Although in the next stage of this progression the suspension falls to F sharp, the dominant 7th is not fully restored because its 5th in the bass is flattened (A flat). To complete the progression, the dominant 7th flattened 5th in resolved in full by Gmajor/minor or partially resolved by Gmaj/min7.

A nice balance is set in this progression between its vertical movements of four individual yet closely grouped chord columns and the contrapuntal play of the lines. The upper voice moves down a step while the lower ones remain stationary. Then the lower lines move under a stationary melody. Notice that the lower lines do not move together but against each other, generating tension at the tritone F sharp-C a moment before relaxation on the major 7th chord.

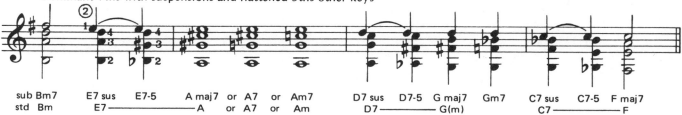

If the required progression lies beyond the twelfth position on the fretboard, the chords may be played at lower positions on higher strings. Unfortunately this necessitates a left-hand overstretch, therefore Ex.185a may be considered as an alternative.

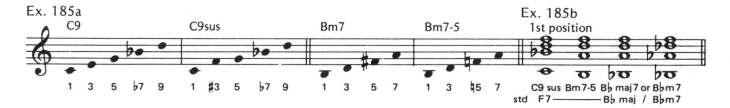

* See also page 85, flattened 5th chord.

From the key chords B flat maj7 or B flat min7 shown in first position, (Ex.185b), the whole progression can be shifted up the fretboard to different key centres. In 3rd position, with the first finger behind the third fret, the chords will centre on Cmaj/min7 — D9sus, D flat min7-5 to Cmaj/min7. In each case the letter names are taken from the bass root notes of the chords.

Minor 7th flattened 5th substitutions

As we have seen, substitutes for minor chords are minor 7ths with the same letter names. In addition, there are other minor 7th substitutes with different letter names and flattened 5ths. These can either substitute the stated minor directly, or be worked in conjunction with its minor 7th (Ex.186).

Ex. 186

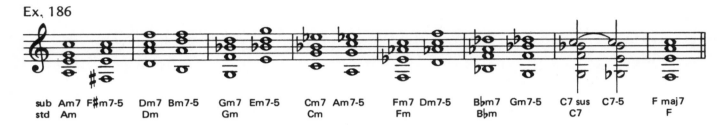

sub	Am7	F#m7-5	Dm7	Bm7-5	Gm7	Em7-5	Cm7	Am7-5	Fm7	Dm7-5	Bbm7	Gm7-5	C7 sus	C7-5	F maj7
std	Am		Dm		Gm		Cm		Fm		Bbm		C7		F

Flattened 5th substitutions for minor and minor 7th chords are found a 6th up from the root of the minor chord in question. If the stated chord is A minor, count up a major 6th from A which is F sharp, and on this note the substitute chord is built. With three notes in common with Amin7 its substitute F sharp min7-5 comprises F sharp, A, its 5th (C sharp) lowered to C and a 7th E. Rather than count up a 6th it's easier to ascertain the position for the shapes of the substitutes by remembering their physical proximity relative to the given minor chords.

Dominant 7ths with flattened 9ths

Another chromatic substitute for a dominant 7th is a dominant 7th with its 9th flattened. In G major the dominant 7th flattened 9th is D7 plus its 9th (E) lowered to E flat (Ex.187a).

Ex. 187a   Ex. 187b

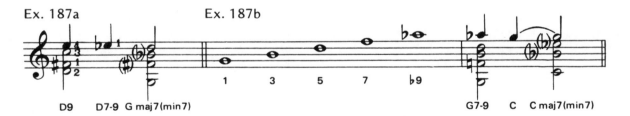

D9   D7-9 G maj7(min7)   1   3   5   7   b9   G7-9   C   C maj7(min7)

With an outer interval a minor 9th (D-E flat), Ex.187a is considerably more piquant than D7 with a diatonic 9th (E). For voice-leading, the natural 9th of the chord is placed in the upper line which then falls to the flattened 9th, and from there into the resolving chord.

A decorated full close in C major/minor, Ex.187b has a dominant 7th flattened 9th comprising G, B, D, F, plus its flattened 9th A flat. If these cadences apply to major keys, their flattened 9ths are chromatic additions. If they apply to minor keys, and they are particularly suited to those, their flattened 9ths are diatonic additions. (In Ex.187b the flattened 9th is a diatonic note in the scale of C minor).

Flattened 5th substitutions

Liaising with or supplanting a dominant 7th, the *flattened 5th substitution* is built on the lowered 2nd degree of the scale. In the key of C major this is the secondary dominant D flat7. Alternatively the chord may be regarded as the dominant built on the flattened 5th note of G7 (Ex.188).*

Ex. 188

Flattened 5th substitution in C major   Guitar chords

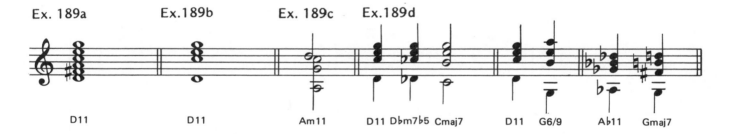

There are two reasons why the 3rd inversion of the flattened 5th chord in Ex.188 and the principal dominant 7th work so well together. Both contain the tritone and so collectively project that interval's leading quality in anticipation of their resolution; they also conduct the voice parts smoothly and mostly by step from the relative minor to the key chord.

Ex.189a introduces the dominant 11th chord. As an extended dominant in relation to G major this is D11, with D, F sharp, A, C, E plus the 11th, G. In conventional harmony the 11th note resolves downwards, G-F sharp. Consequently the 3rd chord note, F sharp, is omitted since this is the resolving note and is therefore not sounded beforehand. Another note frequently omitted from the 11th chord is the 5th, hence Ex.189b. Similarly, minor 7th chords may also have an 11th note superimposed as Ex.189c. Here Amin7 has an upper note D added, denoted in jazz harmony as Am7 (11) or Am11. Ex.189d shows possible resolutions for the 11th chord. In the case of Am11, this may serve as a substitute for Aminor or D7, followed by D7 flattened 5th or A flat major/minor.

In jazz progressions the 11th note of a dominant or minor 7th is often unresolved, in that it is retained with its host chord until the formation is replaced bodily with another harmony, Ex.189d. It should also be noted that in jazz practice too, chord formations denoted as dominant 11ths, (D11), may actually have the same notes as chords named dominant 7th or 9th suspended (D7 sus — D, G, C, E). Therefore, depending upon context and individual definition, some chords with the same notes may be given different symbols.

* The chord formations under discussion may be categorised as follows: as 'extensions' where, for example, G7 is extended with a 9th of 13th; as 'altered' chords such as G7 flattened 5th; or 'substitutions' where D flat7 replaces G7.

Dominant 7ths with diatonic 9ths, altered 9ths and 5ths or their flattened 5th substitutions can be inserted in place of occasional or consecutive dominant 7ths. For example where there are brief or extended passages of secondary dominant 7ths progressing by leaps around the circle of 4ths clock sequence (see Ex.151), their substitutions will allow the parts to descend smoothly in semitone steps Ex.190).

Ex. 190

Flattened 5th and flattened 9th substitutions and extensions

For a closing look at extended chords, they will again be observed in a solo instrumental context, and this time given a rhythmic emphasis. In syncopation their notes are staggered and those normally accented are struck ahead or behind strong beats, and stressed instead on weak beats. Melody notes jump out unpredictably, their attendant harmonies recede. As well as exciting the rhythm, syncopation emphasises the dissonances within the chords, especially when they are denied resolution. The *bossa nova* (new thing) or jazz samba is characterised by syncopated rhythms and extended chords. Its melodies vary in mood from langourous and sentimental to fragmentary and perky, leading or lagging behind their chords, in and out of time with the beat (Ex.191).

Ex. 191 Notturno

Centred on the key chord for the first two bars, the melody then pauses on E while the lower voices step down to B7 suspended. Following their downward inclination, all parts descent together to B flat maj7. Around this chord and B flat7, the melody recalls the pattern set by it a tone above on Cmaj7. After a passing 2nd inversion in bar 8 the bass descends to the root of F sharp min11 — F sharp, A, C sharp omitted, the 7th E and an 11th B. Despite the fact that the bass line descends, the F sharp root is notated in preference to G flat. The latter would complicate matters, calling for the entry of flats and double-flats as the other chord notes. This active discord is partially resolved by the less active Fmin7. From Gminor (bar 10) the bass leaps a perfect 4th to the root of the tonic minor chord, but the harmony passes straight through this to C sharp7. Over another perfect 4th leap to F sharp minor, the melody jumps boldly ahead as an appoggiatura on Gminor. Again the tonic minor is called on and just as quickly dispensed with as the melody is ushered upwards via C sharp dim7 to Dmin7 with an unprepared suspension (see also Ex.166). This suspension is resolved in a traditional manner by the fall of the melody to the 3rd in the chord. Had it fallen a semitone (to F sharp), then the symbol for that chord would have been D7sus. To conclude this sixteen-bar section, Dminor and A flat min11 prepare for the arrival of G7 in a full close re-entry of the tonic chord.

With slight melodic variation the opening phrases are repeated to bar 24 where the melody ascends to E as opposed to its earlier descent to C in bar 8. From bar 25 the melody settles into a recurring pattern, C-D-C, while the bass descends somewhat forlornly to F, and then jumps a diminished 5th to B and from there to the root of the key chord.

While this piece has a discernible key chord, only three times does it strike home with any significance: as the introductory chord, at a half way sectional cadence and as the closing chord. Nonetheless, these are important harmonic bearings, sufficient to establish a tonal anchorage on the note C. By no means, though, does this tonality limit the harmony to a diatonic boundary of C major. That domain is breached with the opening move from Cmaj7 to B7. Physically this entails a mere semitone shift but in theory it is a significant departure from convention. Horizontal voices set the course, not a conventional root progression. Another telling deviation is the chord jump from B flat7 in bar 6. On a traditional basis this chord, a secondary dominant after all, would likely seek the support of its resolving chord E flat major. Instead the bass jumps at a tangent through a tritone B flat to E.

Linking chords on the strength of their individual sounds or linear capabilities rather than to comply with routine sequences, is now widely practised in jazz. It follows a reassessment of harmony which took place around the turn of this century. In the hands of Debussy and Ravel, extended chords acquired an independent existence, unprepared and unresolved. Removed from their familiar contexts, 7th, 9th and 13th chords were heard with fresh interest. No longer contained within diatonic boundaries, these chords, with an infusion of entirely new elements, pointed to the next stage of harmonic transformation, the emancipation of dissonance.

10: RECENT DEVELOPMENTS

Constantly on the move, today's music bourgeons from its past links and through an influx of radically new ideas. Inherited materials and techniques, modified and individually applied, run alongside reactionary trends that reject established principals. Idiomatic distinctions overlap and blur. Formal music seeks the rhythmic vitality and improvisatory freedom of jazz, and jazz had tapped the vast expanse of harmony formulated outside its field. Folk song and mythologies provide the inspiration for compositional structures, mediaeval and Eastern strains seep through musical admixtures, superimposing the past on the present.

Amid these developments, tonality has been at one and the same time rejected, extended and staunchly upheld. Liberated dissonance, the inevitable outcome from the upsurge of chromatic harmony over the late 19th century, pounded this once immutable mainstay of Western composition into dissolution. Over the early decades of the 20th century, radical new techniques anticipated by Josef Matthias Hauer (1883–1959), and formulated by Arnold Schoenberg and his Viennese contemporaries eschewed the supremacy of a single tone and awarded equal status to each of the twelve notes in the chromatic scale. In striving for atonality, new methods for melodic and harmonic organisation were devised. Far from diminishing, this revolution has gained strength and broadened with innumerable offshoots. Such movements, however, have not spelt the suspension of tonality. A long and significant line of established and recent composers have extended tonality in a manner at once individual and innovatory.

It would not be unduly circumspect to approach this bewildering diversity from familiar ground. From there, old patterns can be observed in a modern light, and traditional chords seen flourishing in novel associations and amalgamated with comparative newcomers. No more than a handful of modern resources can be grasped within the space of this chapter but they are those that have occurred with sufficient frequency as to merit them accepted 20th century practices.

Unrelated triad grouping

Lifting well-worn chords from their diatonic habitats is a short step; but one that has accomplished a broad harmonic advance. Their migration may be marginal where just a few alien triads are edged into a closely-knit group traditionally related by key; or with complete disregard to old ties, they cross and intermingle freely in new associations and alignments. In any event, the ear and not the conforms of established patterns determines the order that the chords should follow. And with the most fascinating results: chords with a familiar ring to them no longer sound commonplace.

Ex. 192 Alba

Lento expressivo   Hans Haug

Despite their theoretical disparity, Aminor, Gminor, Eminor and Cmajor contentedly rub shoulders with the diatonic constituents from the key A major. Within this clearly defined key basis a mere sprinkling of unrelated chords hardly casts an old form into a new light; but it does produce subtle harmonic contrast. Listen for the difference in shade and mood between the primary chord harmony in the first bar, and the minor infiltrators in the second. From the usual range of chords in A major, those blends are just not available.

From this tentative mixture of unrelated chords, triads will next be gathered from a wide variety of keys and linked without reference to an overseeing keynote (Ex.193).

Ex. 193

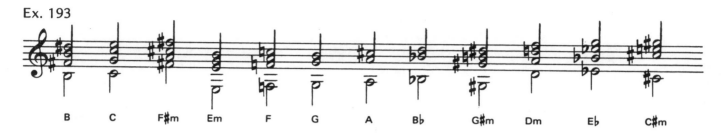

B   C   F#m   Em   F   G   A   Bb   G#m   Dm   Eb   C#m

Provided that Ex.193 evades V-I cadential landmarks and continues with tritone leaps and semitone steps, it could carry on indefinitely without being lured into a recognisable tonality. Free roving across the diatonic ranges shown in Ex.84, accompaniments or harmonic outlines for instrumental compositions may be set from everyday chords in novel progressions. Along a different course, triads will now take the place of single notes in a technique called *parallelism.*

Parallelism

When the same chord is shifted to different pitch levels, it produces a contrasting effect of harmonic ambiguity and melodic clarity (Ex.194).

Ex. 194 Unrelated triads in parallel motion

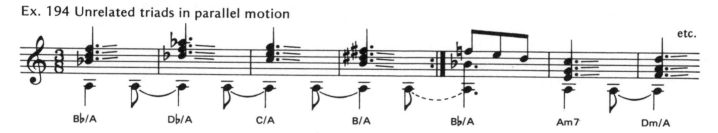

Bb/A   Db/A   C/A   B/A   Bb/A   Am7   Dm/A

If the parallel chords are triads, then the melody they describe is emphasised in that it is reproduced in triplicate. There are two reasons why this creates harmonic vagueness. Since the contour of the melody determines the order of the chords, the more unpredicatable turns the upper line takes, the further removed will that chord procession be from conventional root sequences. Secondly because the chords have a consistent quality and bear equal status, they exert no cadential motions of tension and release. Yet even without a tonic, dominant and leading-note, parallel chords need not necessarily be denied tonality. Though the bass line in Ex.194 does not plot an individual guiding path for the chords, its repeated note acts as a deep-seated reference point for them. At the very beginning of this example the bass A and the triad B flat major conflict with a minor 9th, A-B flat. Four bars later where the first triad is repeated, the parts sound less at variance because the ear has now registered two levels of activity, one encircling the other. An introduction to a song or instrumental piece, Ex.194, may be extended with parallel triads or rounded off cadentially, possibily with the progression in Ex.184, E suspended through E7-5 to Amin7.

Parallelism is not restricted to consecutive triads. Compact multi-layer melodies can be set with 7th chords and all sorts of inversions. These may act as mobile supports for a single melody to weave around, or take over the melodic role from a single line (Ex.195).

Ex. 195 Gigue. Quatre Pieces. No. 4

Jean Absil

Springing from an open-string chord, the melody in Ex.195 suddenly expands from single notes and perfect 4ths into punctuated four-note chordal blocks. Unlike the previous example with parallel concords, these are discords, consecutive dominant 7ths in 3rd inversion with their 5ths raised. The first, in bar 3, is F sharp augmented comprising F sharp, A sharp (B flat), its 5th augmented as D and a 7th E in the bass. This chord is the beginning of a chain of augmented 7ths linking the first two bars to their repeat from bar 7. Then parallel chords again take over, now augmented triads in root position ascending in semitone steps with the melody tapping away between.

Jean Absil

Ex. 196. Quatre Pieces. No. 4

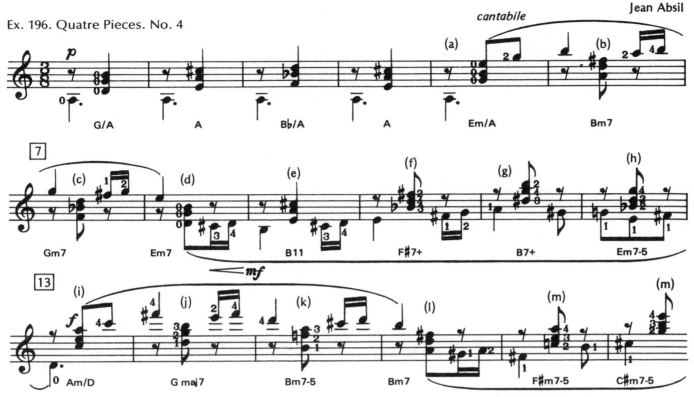

A leisurely introduction of major triads in 2nd inversion sets the pace for a lilting melody which enters first above the chords, and then alternately above and below them. Now there are two viewpoints, vertical and horizontal, from which the relationship of the melody and its interposing chords can be assessed. Vertically, the crotchet melody notes at the beginning of each bar (from bar 6), relate to their accompanying chords as extended notes. From such an understanding, each bar has different chord notes staggered to project a melodic line. Regarding the three minor 7th chords from bar 6, each leads with its root and has its 7th in the bass. For the second phrase (from bar 8), the melody is transferred to the bass. In root position B11 has an 11th E taking the place of its 3rd, D sharp. Following this, F sharp augmented has its 7th in the bass, and its 3rd enharmonically changed from A sharp to B flat. The final chord in this phrase is Emin7 in root position with its 5th (B) flattened.

From bar 13 the melody returns to the upper register, and as before, the chord notes are arranged in deference to it. In 2nd inversion, Gmaj7 has its 7th F sharp in the melody and Bmin7 has its 3rd uppermost and 5th (F sharp) flattened. For the last phrase, the melody is again switched to the bass, beginning with A, the 7th of Bmin7. This line then ascends through the roots of two minor 7th chords in parallel motion.

Horizontally, the melody appears not as a decorative line strung from the notes of extended chords, but as a separate entity veering around a succession of parallel triads. Play the melody only and notice how the first phrase in the treble is balanced by the second phrase in the bass. Similarly, the third phrase, a sequential echo of the first, is balanced by the fourth. Between these lines augmented and inverted triads are shifted bodily. Set in motion by the introductory phrase, 2nd inversion triads continue from (b) to (e). The makeup of the chords then changes from inversions to augmented triads (f) and (g), 1st inversions (a) and (i); and a 2nd inversion (j). The one anomaly is (k), best described as the notated 7th chord. After this is another 2nd inversion (1) and two 1st inversions (m) and (n).

A simple technique in principle and practice, parallelism lends itself readily to the guitar where fluid chord changes can be conducted along the fretboard without involving changes of left-hand fingering. Chords of any size and substance can be utilised and presented in any style. Whatever their manner of execution, be it the florid arpeggiated passages in the preludes of Villa Lobos or the punchy chordal blocks interjecting Wes Montgomery's improvisations, parallelism grants familiar chords a new mobility with melodic clarity.

Quartel harmony

During the diatonic era with its preponderance of 3rd and 6th harmonic building blocks, perfect 4ths persisted, but were bound by pedagogic rules. A 2nd inversion was tolerated provided that its disruptive 4th was flanked by a 3rd or 6th. And many a reproving pencil has marked the spot where consecutive perfect 4ths have inadvertently crept into the lines of a contrapuntal exercise.

A refreshing alternative to 'tertial' chords built from 3rds, *quartel* harmony in perfect 4ths has resurged in 20th century music with a new lease of life. Stark, evocative and archaic it provides just the means to convey ancient and exotic musical imagery. On a broader front, quartel chords have offered modern composers a ready escape from major/minor harmony and its implied progressions. Since the early decades of the 20th century, these elusive and radiant chords have filtered into nearly every conservative and progressive idiom.

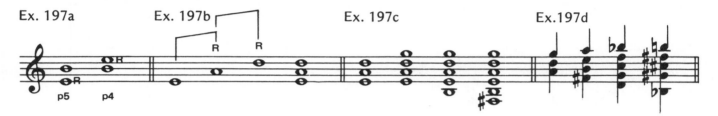

The lower note of the perfect 5th in Ex.197a is the underlying stabiliser or root of that combination. Inverted as a perfect 4th, the upper note becomes the root. When 4ths are superimposed as Ex.197b they cannot collectively stress a single root because two roots are proposed. Neither really wins for their tendency is to cancel each other out. Without a root and with an outer dissonant interval, E to D, Ex.197b is theoretically unstable. In fact its notes merge in an attractive, modern sonority.

Above and below this chord other perfect 4ths are added, extending the formations from three to six notes (Ex.197c). Like triads, fourth-chords can be transferred to different fret positions in parallel motion (Ex.197d). However they are not usually indicated with individual letter names or symbols. As pliable as tertial chords, 4ths can be mounted vertically in solid chord columns, fanned as arpeggios or strung into serrated melodies (Ex.198).

Ex. 198 Prelude IX

Allegretto vivo

Manuel M. Ponce

Over a sustained pedal bass, the upper line in Ex.198 zig-zags in perfect 4ths, G sharp-C sharp, then jumps at tone down to F sharp-B. Though the bass E is the tonal anchor of the phrase, its key signature has no connection with E major. It indicates only those notes that are to be sharpened consistently.

Without diluting their distinctive flavour, fourth-chords can be modified with other intervals. The most compatible additions are those from the same cask, perfect 5ths and octaves. To vary the consistency of these all-perfect interval combinations, 2nds and incidental bass notes can be incorporated (Exs.199).

Ex. 199a   Ex. 199b   Ex. 199c

Ex. 199d

Transferring E from the bass of the quartel chord in Ex.199a to the treble results in a concentration of three different intervals, a perfect 4th A-D, a perfect 5th A-E, and a major 2nd D-E. In Ex.199b three-note fourths are extended by note displacement and octave duplication. Bass separation may also be obtained by major 6th intervals (Ex.199c).

Try incorporating these chords with the melodic improvisation suggested in Ex.31. Shifted spontaneously to different fret positions the three-note chords here can be syncopated with open-bass strings. Also expand the breadth of the harmony now and then with the five and six-note structures given. Perhaps from improvised ventures calculated compositions will emerge. As one example Ex.199d has a clear cut melody against an obscure backround blended from this unique brand of harmony.

Melodic tritone 4ths and 5ths

Pedal notes, leading–notes, IV-I and V-I leaps all help to establish a fixed or passing tonality. But if the aim is to allow the parts of drift of flit unpredictably without direct reference to a central note, then tonality must be consciously deterred, its hold weakened. Neither note in a tritone 4th or 5th is a root. Ambiguous restless intervals, they leave the next move open, urging the melody forward but without giving it a specific sense of direction. A line of successive tritones will leap erratically about, anywhere other than along the path of a conventional.root progression. Even when a central tone presides, a tritone will endeavour to resist its attraction. However brief its opposition may be, a tritone is still distruptive and will create the desired effect of melodic indecision and harmonic ambiguity.

Ex. 200 Mirage (1970)

Allegro

G. Rosetta

Descending in alternating leaps of tritones and perfect 4ths, Ex.200 then levels out through the recurring note C sharp and the steps of the chromatic scale. Now there are certain elements contained in this line's initial descent that try to stave off, however fleetingly, the support of passing roots. These movements merit close attention as they are important characteristics of modern melody and harmony. First, each three-note group leads with an accent. These accents above all else define the melody's minute subdivisions. It is the intervals in the subdivisions particularly those in the first two bars that will be magnified and examined in slow motion. For the present the pedal bass A can be ignored as its significance will be discussed later.

The opening leap of the melody is a tritone, F sharp-C, a diminished 5th. Unlike a perfect 5th which has a root, this dissonance has no root (Exs.201).

Ex. 201a   Ex. 201b   Ex 201c

A perfect 5th is a stable interval, it gives the impression of resting on its lower note, the root of that interval (Ex.201a). Its inversion the perfect 4th is just as relaxed, stabilised by its upper note or root. Tritone 4ths and 5ths have no such repose. Even when the lower note of the diminished 5th in Ex.201b is given a headstart to assert a root, that note is contested and neutralised by the opposing upper note.

Returning to the beginning of Ex.200, magnified in Ex.201c, its opening tritone leap lacks stability. However the next leap, a perfect 4th, does have a root. So despite its shaky start, this group lands with its second leap on solid ground momentarily stabilised by its upper note B. Turning to the next note group, the reverse procedure takes place. Where earlier a tritone took the lead and was then resolved, this tritone must await resolution from the first note in the third group (Ex.202).

Ex. 202 Second note group

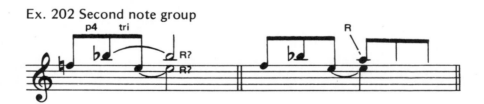

Then the latter tritone thwarts the three notes from associating with a root. Though this group begins with one, it is dispelled by the ensuing tritone. And so on throughout the first two bars: within each three-note group, brief decisive leaps alternate with faltering ones. Only in the last bar does the melody really engage a root, its pedal A which endeavoured to take hold at the beginning of the phrase. Fortified with perfect 4ths and 5ths, A serves not only as the root for the notes in its vicinity, but turns out to be the tonal note for the whole phrase. Hovering in the background for most of the activity, it is then brought to the fore by the upward semitone through G sharp and the perfect intervals in the arpeggio above.

Active intervals, tritone 4ths and 5ths urge the melody forward without committing it to a predictable goal. Consequently, a section of a melody composed of consecutive tritones or equally mobile 7th and 9th intervals would pursue an angular indeterminate tack. If, on top of this, its rhythm is irregular, then its gestures would be so much more erratic. On the other hand, perfect 4ths and 5ths have in-built stability and 3rds and 6ths seek triadic unity. Between these extremes, an overall balance is often sought whereby unsettled sections are compensated by moments of comparative or complete repose (Ex.203).

Ex. 203 Cuatro Tientos

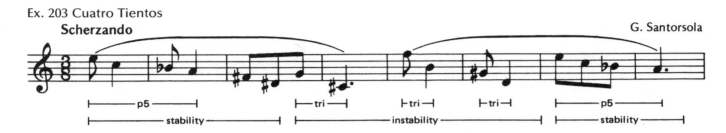

Over its inital descent Ex.203 is given the stability of a root, the note A, and a harmonic association, the triad Aminor. From this conventional departure the melody undergoes some unusual turns, encompassing during its course the total range of the chromatic scale A-A. Unlike a traditional opening four-bar statement which is usually contained with a cadence, this phrase pauses restlessly on the lower note of a tritone. And just as restlessly the following phrase responds with two tritone leaps and a 9th. At the end of the phrase, the melody again descends through the arpeggio Aminor which restores its former stability.

Ex. 204 Canzone Notturna (1969)

As it happens the beginning of Ex.204 also has a harmonic association notwithstanding its prominent tritone and minor 7th leap. Regroup the notes vertically and a 9th chord emerges: C9 — C, E, B flat (A sharp), D. With two 3rds, C-E and B flat-D, this chord needs no 5th to establish a root since the 5th (G) is implied. In a conventional setting C9 would likely be followed by F major or a chord with an F bass. Evading this obvious formula the melody descends with passing allusions to the triads Emajor (E-G sharp) and Eminor (E-G), to pause irresolute after its tritone leap, B-F. After this tritone's inversion (F—B), the melody's spell of uncertainty is broken by a sudden and consistent rhythmic acceleration. Impelled through the arpeggio E7, the melody would, on a traditional course, centre on the chord Amajor. Aware of such a rut the composer avoids it. Anyway, a cadential break at this juncture would be unduly arresting, and not least, out of style. To maintain ambiguity and thereby leave a choice of melodic outlets open, another tritone with a major 2nd is inserted in the adjoining chord.

Harmonic tritones in altered-fourth chords

Chords with tritones are of course nothing new; dominant 7ths, diminished 7ths and augmented 6ths all contain tritones. But so familiar are these chords that their tritones channel the voice parts into predictable resolutions rather than broaden their scope. Tritones in recent chord structures are quite a different matter. Combined with perfect 4ths, perfect 5ths, and 2nds or 9ths they merge and conflict without indicating the direction of their next move (Ex.205).

Ex. 205 Prelude XII
Moderato

Manuel M. Ponce

Two modern techniques distract this passage from the overall key basis of the piece, F sharp minor. First is its parallel chord progression and second is the tritones and diminished octaves within those chords. Though the excerpt opens with a standard chord, Emajor in 1st inversion — G sharp, B, E, this is soon obscured by the diminished 5th, E sharp-B. Taken down a semitone the pattern for the first arpeggio is reversed over the second half of the bar. Similiarly the arpeggios in bar 2 follow the same sequence, rising or falling with each downward step in the bass. Such a diffusion of consecutive tritones and perfect 4ths totally blots out the key basis established over the bars beforehand. Veering back to the keynote, the leading-note E sharp hints at its imminent arrival and the dominant to tonic leap in the bass reinstates it.

Altered - fourth chords

Ex. 206a   Ex. 206b   Ex. 206c Ex. 206d   Ex. 206e   Ex. 206f   Ex. 206g

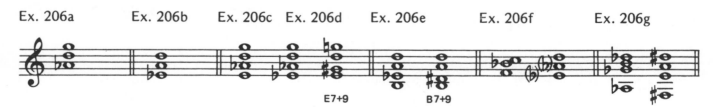

Considerably more piquant than perfect-fourth chords, Exs.206 comprise perfect 4ths and tritone or *altered 4ths*. In Ex.206a the altered 4th is the lower interval A flat-D. Ex.206b has an altered 4th E flat-A, and Exs.206c-d are extensions of the foregoing chords. As a point of interest Ex.206c can be analysed as a dominant 7th raised 9th: E7+9 — E, G, sharp, (B), D, plus its 9th (F sharp) raised to G. Ex.206e is another raised 9th shape: B7+9 — B, D sharp, (F sharp), A with its 9th (C sharp) raised to D. Both shapes are moveable and take their letter names from their bass notes. In a dominant role these altered 9th chords will substitute dominant 7ths: B7+9 to B9 to B7-9 where the upper voice falls from D through C sharp to C.

In contrary motion, Ex.206f has a modified fourth-chord linked to an altered-fourth chord: E flat, A, D, or E flat, A flat, D as preferred. Also in contrary motion but with four parts, Ex.206g has an 11th chord joined to an altered-fourth chord. All shapes are moveable, and with perfect-fourth chords may be spontaneously shifted to different fret positions. For added variety, fourth-chords can be amalgamated with minor 7th, 11ths, dominant 7ths with suspensions and major 7ths (Ex.207).

Ex. 207 Nuance   L.B.

On a V-I and stepwise bass line, tertial chords with perfect and tritone 4ths merge into a hazy background for a distinct and flowing melody. Continued from Ex.182 but beginning with (a) and not the Amaj7 chord concluding that example, the centre voices in consecutive 4ths tap a samba-like pulse to contrast the more sustained sweeps of the upper line. In bar 2 the outer lines fall to (b), completing A flat min11 (see Ex.189c). While the two upper lines hold, the lower ones fall a semitone to (c) or G7-5 where the flattened 5th, D flat, is uppermost. By contrary motion the lower lines fall a semitone to (d) and the melody rises to the augmented 5th of F sharp7. In partial resolution the melody falls to C sharp the 5th of its accompanying chord. Two more extended chords follow: (e) as B11 and (f) as Gmaj7. From the fourth bar onwards perfect and tritone 4ths preponder: (g) is a fourth-chord with an incidental bass note; (h) is a modified fourth-chord; (i) is an altered-fourth chord with an incidental bass; (j) is a perfect-fourth chord; (k) is a perfect-fourth chord when its adjoining melody note D is added; and (1) is an altered-fourth chord.

Ex. 208

Theme moderato   L. Berkeley

The opening phrase of a theme for a set of variations, Ex.208 is embellished with two arpeggiated figurations composed of perfect and tritone 4ths. An abrupt introductory chord agitated by a tritone sets the melody off on a loose diatonic basis, the scale B minor. With tritones obscuring the harmony, the keynote of the melody is not clarified until bar 4 where its leading-note A sharp and dominant bass F sharp signal its arrival. Regarding the arpeggio at the end of bar 2, this has two perfect 4ths with a tritone between. From its upper note the melody leaps a perfect 4th to F sharp then falls a tone to E. Echoing this pattern but from a slightly lower level, the melody descends after the next altered-fourth chord from C sharp to B. Approaching the end of the phrase, the line leaps a minor and major 3rd then steadies on two crotchets to end on its keynote B.

Enigmatic combinations, perfect and altered-fourth chords blend in a variety of shades and are adaptable to different styles. Hand in glove with extended chords or integrated with diatonic melodies, they enrich existing harmony and add to it a radiantly new dimension.

Counterpoint

Liberated from conventional chord sequences, 20th century counterpoint indulges in melodic and rhythmic freedom. Each part is treated individually, contributing to the flow of its neighbouring lines or contradicting them in extemes of grating dissonance. Rhythm, too, has been emancipated, breaking away from its three and four-beat uniformity. Bar lines, those once dictatorial markers for rhymed phrasing and regulated accents, if not discarded, have become far more flexible. Instead of pacing the accent they now bow to it, continously shifting to accommodate complex note groupings and ever-changing time signatures.

Parallel with these innovations, traditional crafts and designs endure. Though the strands of modern counterpoint liaise and recoil outside established harmonic schemes, symmetry and its balance of statement and response is still much in evidence. Expanding tonality has not totally jettisoned its cadential links. Cadences, however concealed and diminished in authority, nonetheless continue to guide the lines around passing or resting tonalities.

Consonant intervals, and come to that, concords are not necessarily inanimated. Dissonances are not always active — they can take a neutral stance. The effect of a particular consonance or dissonance in counterpoint can only be truly weighed when other factors, rhythmic impetus, dynamics, the directional thrust of the lines, are taken into account. A measure of these fundamentals will prepare for a later, more advanced study of 20th century counterpoint.

Ex. 209 Ocram

Angelo Gilardino

The germinal idea or motif from which Ex.209 is developed is the melodic and rhythmic pattern in the first bar. In this case the motif has a harmonic core, the triad Cminor in root position. Though the root of this chord is reinforced by its repeat and the octave G, it is undermined by the melody's leap of a tritone and an augmented octave. So what we hear is a melody that begins from a solid basis only to expand in disarray. Vertical and horizontal stability is restored in the second bar by the return of the triad and the root's repeat. Despite another assailing tritone, the root endeavours to hold its ground, for it now has a perfect 5th and octave rallying to its support.

On divergent paths, the two upper lines enter bar three where they halt abruptly on a prominent discord. This discord has a twofold purpose: it emphasises the melody's peak and erases all trace of the motif so as to clear the air for the single line to exert itself as an individual entity. Stressed with asymmetrical accents, 5/8, 7/8, 6/8 and eluding root relationships, the line falls erratically and then rises to rest on B under which a variant of the motive is heard. Rhythmically consistent but melodically altered, a brief root is established in this motif through G-D, and is just as soon cancelled by F sharp and G sharp. Across the last bar two roots take hold: first is the earlier note C, proposed by G in the upper line. This, however, is ousted by the tritone A flat-D, whose upper note is also the upper note of the forthcoming 5th. To complete this interval the centre line falls to G, and on that note the centre line rests, and the section ends.

Then tension and ambiguity is created by tritones, 2nds, 7ths and altered octaves. It may be conveyed vertically with harmonic intervals or horizontally with melodic intervals. Provided that perfect 4ths and 5ths are given time to assert themselves and are not overpowered by accompanying dissonances, they will check instability.

Ex. 210

In Ex.210 two lines conflict across an array of intervals which, far from snatching at passing roots, try to establish two contesting tonalities. In isolation, the bass line can be heard as a lyrical figure rising from C (a dominant) through E (a leading-note) to F (a tonic). But this so-called tonic is irreconcilable with the upper harmonic group, a triad E flat major in 2nd inversion — B flat, E flat, G flat, where the lower interval of a perfect 4th suggests a root E flat.

Ex. 211

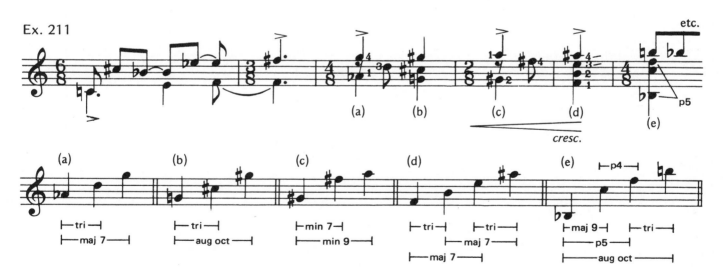

Four factors combine to produce the climatic discord at (d), Ex.211. First are the accents from which the upper line rebounds during its ascent; second is the increasing volume and the air of expectancy it generates; third is the cumulating dissonance resulting from the expansion of two voices to four; and finally the culminating tension at (d) is sustained for the duration of a crotchet. A shorter note value would deny that tension its full impact. Without diluting the plangency of the parts, a goal quite unforseen is reached. The two centre voices, spaced at a perfect 4th, suggest a root but underlying this is another more firmly implanted. This is B flat proposed by two perfect 5ths one within the chord, and the other, the leap of the bass, F-B flat.

Ex. 212

FALSE RELATIONS

L.B.

What may appear outwardly a revolutionary trend often has many evolutionary elements. The dissonances peppering 'False Relations' are certainly modern in treatment and texture, but there are facets to its overall design that are elemental. For one, the opening motifs are nub of the piece, from these the lines develop and return to, before venturing forth again. Statement and response is fundamental to musical design and takes many forms, not always in equal proportions. A gradually ascending line can be offset by its most fleeting descent. Incremental build-ups of tension are sometimes countered by a single interval or chord at rest. Echoes, sequences, a fair distribution of consonance and dissonance all contribute towards balance; they are structural factors common to music of all periods and styles.

This chapter has traced a few of the many harmonic vagaries outside the reaches of the major and minor scales. Yet many of the rudiments encountered earlier within the diatonic field have since appeared in new guises. Triads belong as much in contemporary forms as they did to the music of Bach. The same intervals are used now as then, and, in folk song and popular music, the same chord progressions too. So it is hardly a matter of sampling those basic ingredients and then dismissing them in favour of others entirely novel. Where changes were pointed out they lay not in the components themselves but in the individuality and freedom exercised with their assembly. When the opportunity arose, the same device was evaluated in two or more contrasting styles, sometimes with centuries between them. The idea behind this approach was to show how musical materials could be moulded to produce a variety of effects. If, on the way it has provided an understanding of harmony from the past, and prompted further enquiry into music of the present, this book has served its purpose.

MUSICAL TERMS

accelerando	growing faster
adagio	slowly
ad libitum	freely
agitato	restless
al fine	to the end
alla	in the style of
alla breve	(¢) cut time: two beats to the bar.
allegretto	a bright tempo but slower than allegro
allegro	fast
andante	moderately slow but flowing
andantino	a little faster than andante
animato	with spirit
annular	(a) third finger (right hand)
assai	very
a tempo	in the original tempo
attacca	without pausing
bravura	boldness
brio	vigour
cadenza	a solo passage often unaccompanied
calando	gradually softer and slower
cantabile	in a singing style
capriccioso	fanciful, capricious
coda	a closing passage
con, col	with
crescendo	increasing in volume or loudness
da, dal	from
da capo	(D.C.) from the beginning
D.C. al fine	from the beginning to the word Fine (finish)
dal segno	(D.S.) from the sign %
diminuendo	gradually softer
dolce	sweetly
dolcissimo	very sweetly
doloroso	sadly
energico	vigorous
espressivo	expressively
fermata	(⌒) pause
finale	the concluding movement
fine	the end
forte	(f) loud
forte-piano	(fp) accent strongly then diminishing to piano
fortissimo	(ff) very loud
forzando	(fz) a note or chord strongly accented
giusto	in strict time
glissando	slurred, in a gliding manner
grace notes	ornamental notes
grazioso	gracefully
gruppetto	a group of grace notes.
il	the
indice	(i) first finger (right hand)
largamente	in a full, broad style
larghetto	slowly, but not as slowly as largo
largo	a slow, broad tempo
legato	connecting the notes smoothly by slurs
leggiero	lightly
lento	slow
ma	but
ma non troppo	but not too much
maestoso	majestic, dignified
maggiore	major key
marcato	marked and emphatic

marcia	march
medio	(*m*) middle finger (right hand)
meno	less
meno mosso	less motion, slower
mezzo	half
mezzo forte	(*mf*) moderately loud
mezzo piano	(*mp*) moderately soft
minore	minor key
misterioso	mysteriously
moderato	moderately
molto	much, very
mordent	an embellishment of two or more notes played as a short trill
morendo	dying away, softer and softer
mosso	movement
moto	motion
non	not
obbligato	a counter melody which complements the theme
opus	a work or composition
ossia	otherwise; or else; indicating another way of playing the passage
ottava	(*8va*) to be played an octave higher
passionato	passionate
patetico	pathetic
pause	⌢ a pause also called a fermata
pianissimo	(*pp*) very soft
piano	(*p*) softly
più	more
più mosso	more movement, faster
poco a poco	little by little
prestissimo	as fast as possible
presto	very fast; faster than allegro
primo	(*1mo*) first, as tempo primo
pulgar	(*p*) thumb (right hand)
quasi	like; in the style of
rallentando	(*rall.*) gradually slower
rinforzando	(*rfz.*) reinforced: with added emphasis
risoluto	resolutely
ritardando	(*rit.*) retarding: gradually slowing the tempo
ritenuto	(*riten.*) in a slower tempo: held back
rubato	robbing or taking from the notes their strict time value by hurrying or retarding for the purpose of expression
scherzando	playfully
semplice	in a simple manner
sempre	always
senza	without
sforzando	(*sfz*) with sudden force or emphasis
simile	in a like manner
smorzando	extinguished; suddenly dying away
sostenuto	sustained
sotto voce	in a quiet, subdued tone
spirito	spirit, with energy
staccato	detached, cut short
stringendo	accelerating the tempo
stresso	same
subito	immediately
tacet	silence: do not play
tenuto	*(ten.)* held for the full time value
tranquillo	quietly, calmly
trill	a rapid alternation between the printed note and the adjacent note
troppo	too much
tutti	all together
vivace	lively, briskly
vivo	animated, quick
volti subito	*(v.s.)* turn the page immediately

Index

8/91 (12125)